DESIGNING PROFESSIONAL PORTFOLIOS
for Change

Kay Burke, Ph.D.

IRI SkyLight
TRAINING AND PUBLISHING, INC.
Arlington Heights, Illinois

Grateful acknowledgment is made to the following for use of copyrighted work:

Figure 2.4, "Innovations Compared to Objectives," appeared as Figure 2.2 on page 25 of *Results: The Key to Continuous School Improvement* by Mike Schmoker. Alexandria, VA.: Association for Supervision and Curriculum Development. Copyright 1996 ASCD. Reprinted with permission. All rights reserved.

Figure 5.3, "Coaching/Evaluation Distinctions," appeared as Figure 2.1 on page 14 of *Cognitive Coaching: A Foundation for Renaissance Schools* by Arthur L. Costa and Robert J. Garmston. Copyright ©1994 by Christopher-Gordon Publishers, Inc. Reprinted with permission.

Figure 8.4, "Samples of Expected Teacher Competencies," appeared in *The Clearing House,* vol. 66, no. 4, pp. 235–237, March–April 1993. Reprinted with permission of the Helen Dwight Reid Educational Foundation. Published by Heldref Publications. Copyright ©1993.

Blackline master "Evaluation of Portfolio" appeared as Figure 6.6 on page 78 of *Enhancing Professional Practice: A Framework for Teaching* by Charlotte Danielson. Copyright ©1996 by Charlotte Danielson. Reprinted with permission from the author.

Designing Professional Portfolios for Change

Published by IRI/SkyLight Training and Publishing, Inc.
2626 S. Clearbrook Dr., Arlington Heights, IL 60005
800-348-4474 or 847-290-6600
Fax 847-290-6609
info@iriskylight.com
http://www.iriskylight.com

Creative Director: Robin Fogarty
Managing Editor: T. B. Zaban
Editors: Edward Roberts, Dara Lee Howard
Proofreader: Jennifer Gillis
Graphic Designer: Heidi Ray
Cover and Illustration Designer: David Stockman
Type Compositors: Donna Ramirez, Christina Georgi
Production Supervisor: Bob Crump

LCCCN 96-80215
ISBN 1-57517-056-6

1906C-5-98V
Item Number 1488
06 05 04 03 02 01 00 99 98   15 14 13 12 11 10 9 8 7 6 5 4 3

Dedication

To my husband Frank,
my mother Lois Brown,
and all the Brown and Burke family members
in the United States and Ireland.

Contents

Foreword

Designing Professional Portfolios for Change represents a breakthrough in conventional thinking about how to change teaching practice. Many outstanding teachers use the process informally, but change in practice is facilitated for an individual through the various reflective activities described by Burke.

The increased demand for accountability has placed another burden on already overloaded school administrators. Giving teachers the tools and inviting them to become full partners in a continuous improvement process is a significant shift in thinking about who is responsible and must be in charge of the improvement process. The burden for improvement can now be a shared responsibility, with classroom teachers participating in determining the what and how of their own professional growth. This new approach will foster the collaboration and collegiality that is essential to building a professional environment. In addition, this process directs greater attention to establishing a purpose for change and puts the students at the center. Too much energy has been spent in the past on "change for change's sake"—this approach has seldom been effective.

Professional portfolios enable classroom teachers to take responsibility for their professional growth. The activities and information contained in this book will guide teachers and administrators through the steps and important considerations. The result, for those who are serious about improving student learning, will be exciting and rewarding.

Teachers who commit to this process will be impressed with what they discover about themselves. The insights they glean will enable them to better assess their readiness for change and innovation in educational practice. Going through the portfolio process will also enable teachers to have a better grasp of what their students are going through as they develop their portfolios.

We are overdue in recognizing that practices in the past for promoting change have had very little success. *Designing Professional Portfolios for Change* is the long-awaited answer to a number of complex and difficult problems that surround assessment practice. The future for those who embark on this path is uncertain. But we know that unless teachers are a major part of the evaluation process, little will truly change. This would be unfortunate for the nation's future.

Kay Burke has a long and successful career in developing alternative and authentic assessment plans. This latest contribution builds on the successful work she has done and breaks new ground in the educational profession.

PHILLIP HARRIS
Phi Delta Kappa

Acknowledgments

"A journey of a thousand miles must begin with a single step." —Lao-tzu

Professional development is a journey. When I started researching professional portfolios three years ago, I started with a single step. I compiled my own portfolio. The experience of sorting through what I collected, reflecting on what I learned, and sharing my insights with colleagues was powerful. I was ready to continue the journey.

Writing this book has been a tremendous learning experience and an adventure. I would like to thank the following people who have contributed their ideas, insights, and support throughout the process.

- Jim Bellanca and Robin Fogarty of IRI/SkyLight Publishing for emphasizing the need to make the whole process meaningful and manageable for teachers and administrators;

- Kris Knudsen, Pam Lindberg, Jo Nancy Warren, the "volunteer" teachers from District #21 in Wheeling, Illinois, and the student teachers from Illinois State University for working with me for a year to develop their portfolios;

- Phil Harris, Cindy Whalen, and Roz Brown for modeling long-term professional development and for epitomizing educational professionalism;

- The facilitators, teachers, and students enrolled in the Field-Based Master's Program sponsored by IRI/SkyLight and Saint Xavier University for experimenting with professional portfolios;

- Barbara Harold, Heidi Ray, Donna Ramirez, Dave Stockman, Dara Lee Howard, and the rest of the IRI/SkyLight Publishing staff for being creative and patient throughout the production of this book; and

- My friends, co-workers, and professional colleagues for encouraging me throughout "Kay's Excellent Portfolio Adventure."

KAY BURKE
January 1997

Introduction

"A Professional Development Portfolio provides teachers with a framework for initiating, planning, and facilitating their personal/professional growth while building connections between their interests and goals and those of the school." (Dietz 1991, Facilitator's Guide, section 1)

Professional Portfolios

To make student assessment more authentic, educators have begun using student portfolios to capture evidence of growth and development over time. Teachers are now asking students to reflect on their learnings, share their findings with peers, and set new goals based upon their strengths and weaknesses. Many educators, students, and parents find that portfolios show a dimension of the students' learning that is often not found in traditional and standardized tests. The portfolio is more personalized, allowing choice and encouraging reflection.

As teachers find success using portfolios with their own students, they realize that portfolios can provide clearer representations of themselves as professionals than the traditional twenty-minute observation by the principal each spring. As Wolf (1996, 34) states, "Although portfolios can be time-consuming to construct and cumbersome to review, they also can capture the complexities of professional practice in ways that no other approach can. Not only are they an effective way to assess teaching quality, but they also provide teachers with opportunities for self-reflection and collegial interactions based on documented episodes of their own teaching."

Educators have begun to explore the various uses of professional portfolios in documenting teaching practice. They have also begun to reexamine current staff development practices such as inservices to determine whether they facilitate long-term teacher learning and promote student achievement. As Sykes (1996, 465) states, "Teacher learning must be the heart of any effort to improve education in our society."

Inservices

Imagine hiring a basketball coach to come in once a month and advise players he has never seen play. He doesn't know their strengths and weaknesses, but he still prescribes the plays they should use. Eisner (1991) uses this analogy to describe inservice programs in most schools. Someone is brought in to say something about curriculum, the teaching process, classroom management, or assessment. This person has never observed the teaching of the teachers to whom she is speaking; therefore, she hardly takes into account their individual strengths and weaknesses.

Usually the information offered in inservice programs is general because it has to meet the needs of K–12 teachers in areas ranging from first grade reading to twelfth grade physics. Eisner (1991, 12) says, "The instructors would need to be clairvoyant to know what advice might be appropriate for individual teachers."

The more generic the presentations, the larger the audience, the shorter the time period, the fewer chances for transfer. How many times have teachers left this type of "inservice du jour" and said, "Yes, but—I teach special education children and this doesn't apply to me," or "It will never work with the group I have this year," or "Obviously, the consultant has never taught 'high school'."

Furthermore, Shanker (1996, 223) says the sums most school districts in the United States invest in continuing teacher development are paltry compared to what American business spends on continuing the education of its employees. Moreover, the dollars that are spent are not spent wisely. Shanker says, "They go mostly for one-shot workshops devoted to the reform of the month, chosen by others and unconnected to the needs of students and teachers."

The sums most school districts in the United States invest in continuing teacher development are paltry compared to what American business spends on continuing the education of its employees.

Professional Development

"Our society can no longer accept the hit-or-miss hiring, sink-or-swim induction, trial-and-error teaching, and take-it-or-leave-it professional development it has tolerated in the past." —What Matters Most: Teaching for America's Future *as cited in Bradley 1996b, p. 14*

Professional development has been described as a lifelong process whereby an individual strives to deepen his knowledge base, hone his skills, sharpen his judgment, stay current with new developments in the field, and experiment with innovations that promise improvements in practice (Sykes, in Elmore 1990).

Bellanca (1995, 6) defines individual professional development as a decision to expand one's repertoire of knowledge or skills. A teacher may select a graduate program, workshop, conference, action research project, or visitation to another school to grow professionally. Bellanca defines a school system's professional development program as "a planned, comprehensive, and systemic program designed to improve all school personnel's ability to design, implement, and assess productive change in each individual and in the school organization."

Shanker (1996, 223) says that for professional development to be effective, "It must offer serious intellectual content, take explicit account of the various contexts of teaching and experiences of teachers, offer support for informed dissent, be ongoing and embedded in the purposes and practices of schooling, help teachers to change within an environment that is often hostile to change, and involve teachers in defining the purposes and activities that take place in the name of professional development."

Staff Development

Many people use the terms "professional development" and "staff development" interchangeably, but Bellanca (1995, 6) argues that staff development is "the effort to correct teaching deficiencies by providing opportunities to learn new methods of classroom management and instruction or to 'spray paint' the district with hoped-for classroom innovations."

Many people argue that staff development as it is now practiced does not encompass the potential for long-term application and transfer that professional development offers. And even when inservice and staff development plans are called "professional development," they often do not involve long-term commitments of time, energy, and resources, nor do they allow for any personal choice. Also, most staff development does not focus on developing long-term goals and on mediating continuous growth and development to deepen one's "knowledge, skills, and judgment"—qualities Sykes describes as being the hallmark of professional development.

Obviously, there are some outstanding examples of staff development being implemented in schools and districts. The perception of many educators, parents, and reform analysts, however, is that staff development usually means one-shot inservice days strategically placed throughout the year almost like "parachute drops" of the district's hot topics or the state's new mandates. Despite the intentions and efforts of the staff development coordinator, participants often feel that inservice programs do not meet their needs. Sadly, the information presented in these mandated inservices is *presented to all, appreciated by some,* and *used by few.*

As Fullan and Stiegelbauer (1991, 315) state, "Nothing has promised so much and has been so frustratingly wasteful as the thousands of workshops and conferences that led to no significant change in practice when the teachers returned to their classroom." In fact, the research of Joyce shows that when trainers present a theory and model new ideas, eighty-five percent of the audience understands the concept, fifteen to eighteen percent attain the skill, but only five to ten percent ever apply what they learn in their own classroom unless they engage in long-term peer coaching. Research by Joyce and Showers indicates that it may take up to twenty follow-up and coaching sessions to ensure the successful implementation of a particular teaching strategy. In other words, there is a meager relationship

Staff development as it is now practiced does not encompass the potential for long-term application and transfer that professional development offers.

between components of training and levels of impact (National Staff Development Council and National Association of Secondary School Principals Study Guide 1995, 31).

In addition, the "top down" structure of district-wide staff development does not allow the individual to make decisions and to try to solve problems meaningful to him. The very mention of staff development conveys the impression of something done *to* teachers and *to* students rather than something done *by* teachers *for* students. Cameron (1996, 226) is concerned about the hierarchy of decision makers who mandate the one-size-fits-all approaches that do not serve students. "Only teachers and administrators prepared to make judgments about students and what they need to achieve can help students achieve quality learning outcomes." The Venn diagram in Figure 1 compares some of the perceived differences between the current practice of staff development and the emerging practice of professional development.

The very mention of staff development conveys the impression of something done to teachers and to students rather than something done by teachers for students.

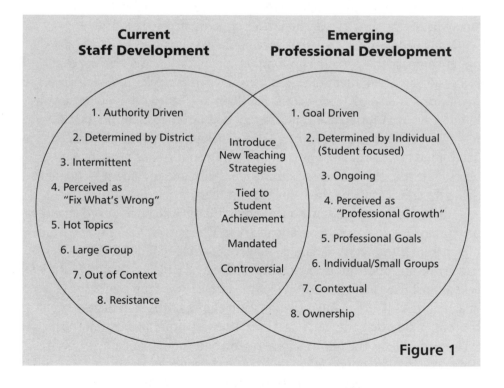

Current Staff Development

1. Authority Driven
2. Determined by District
3. Intermittent
4. Perceived as "Fix What's Wrong"
5. Hot Topics
6. Large Group
7. Out of Context
8. Resistance

Introduce New Teaching Strategies

Tied to Student Achievement

Mandated

Controversial

Emerging Professional Development

1. Goal Driven
2. Determined by Individual (Student focused)
3. Ongoing
4. Perceived as "Professional Growth"
5. Professional Goals
6. Individual/Small Groups
7. Contextual
8. Ownership

Figure 1

Professional Development Plan

In their quest for substantive professional development, many teachers around the country have developed professional development plans (PDPs) to target goals they want to achieve for a one- to three-year period. They then can use any combination of the professional development types listed in Figure 2 to document their progress in achieving their goals. Often they decide upon their plan after conferring with peers, mentors, or supervisors who become informal or formal partners. One advantage of this program is that it allows educators some flexibility in achieving their goals.

Types of Professional Development

Interactive Activities

- Internet
- Workshops
- School Visits
- Conferences
- Summer Institutes
- Team Teaching
- Network Memberships

Investigative Strategies

- Educational Journals
- Educational Books
- Training Manuals
- Individual Action Research
- Group Action Research
- Videos of Best Practices
- Computer Programs
- Sabbaticals
- Fellowships

Formal Programs

- University Courses
- Degree Programs
- Professional Development Schools
- National Board for Professional Teaching Standards
- Training Academies
- Licensure Standards for Teachers
- Licensure Standards for Administrators

Reflective Practices

- Log Entries
- Reflective Journals
- Videotaped Lessons
- Peer Coaching
- Mentoring
- Self-Evaluations
- Professional Development Plans
- Professional Portfolios

Figure 2

For example, one teacher may decide to explore Gardner's theory of multiple intelligences in his classroom over a two-year period in order to help students increase academic achievement. As part of his plan, he could devise the following strategy:

Professional Goals

1. Read books by Gardner, Armstrong, Lazear, Chapman, and Campbell on multiple intelligences.

2. Read relevant articles in educational journals.

3. Visit a teacher who uses multiple intelligences centers.

4. Attend a conference on multiple intelligences.

5. Create lessons designed to address the intelligences.

6. Create authentic assessments to measure the intelligences.

7. Graph students' achievement in classwork and on standardized tests.

He would then develop specific learner-centered goals to show how students benefit from his efforts to incorporate multiple intelligences into his teaching.

One way the teacher can document his steps to achieve the stated goals is by collecting artifacts in a portfolio. The portfolio would contain a variety of examples: annotated bibliographies of the books and articles he has read; pictures from the classroom that depicted multiple intelligences centers; programs from the conferences he attended; sample lessons he created; copies of tests, rubrics, or portfolio assignments he used to assess students' use of the intelligences; records of students' test scores; and an analysis of students' questionnaires. The teacher would also make comments throughout the portfolio, describing the entries and reflecting on what he has learned about his teaching and the students' learnings. Without these commentaries and reflections, as Wolf (1996) warns us, the portfolio is no more than a "scrapbook of mementos."

One way the teacher can document his steps to achieve the stated goals is by collecting artifacts in a portfolio.

Types of Professional Portfolios

"Portfolios have much to offer the teaching profession. When teachers carefully examine their own practices, those practices are likely to improve." (Wolf 1996, 37)

Preservice

"Over half the teachers teaching in the year 2005 will have been hired in the preceding decade" (Darling-Hammond 1996, 6). Many colleges and universities are revamping their programs to prepare students for the challenges of teaching in the years ahead. Darling-Hammond (1996, 9) recommends making the investment up front of selecting, training, and supporting beginning teachers in order to control the cost incurred through incompetence. "These early investments will also reduce the costs of band-aid approaches to staff development for those who have not learned to teach effectively and the costs of remediation, or trying to dismiss poor teachers—not to mention the costs of compensating for the effects of their poor teaching on children."

Many colleges are incorporating portfolios in their education programs to showcase students' learnings, share reflections, and make connections between the college classroom and elementary, middle, and high school classrooms. Some colleges use the portfolio primarily as a reflection tool, while others use it to document specific competencies. Professors at the University of Memphis require student teachers to keep portfolios to document demographic data and placement conferences; to conduct performance reviews in six areas—(1) planning, (2) communication, (3) leadership, (4) teaching strategies, (5) classroom management, and (6) evaluation—to perform a self-rating; to showcase evidence from at least five observations; and to showcase unit lesson plans, sample lesson plans, work samples, and daily logs (Chance and Rakes 1994, 1–3).

Professors at the College of Education at Wayne State University in Detroit developed a portfolio process for documenting development in ten areas. They want evidence showing that the student teacher: (1) knows academic content and a variety of teaching methods; (2) organizes and implements effective instructional programs; (3) demonstrates appropriate classroom management techniques to ensure a safe and orderly environment conducive to learning; (4) stimulates students' creative and critical thinking; (5) has knowledge of human growth and development; (6) is committed to students and their learning; (7) uses listening, speaking, reading, and writing skills effectively; (8) behaves in an ethical, reflective and professional manner; (9) understands the importance of multicultural perspectives; and (10) applies appropriate assessment, evaluation, and testing procedures (Synder et al. 1993, 56). Student teachers have a half-hour interview to discuss their portfolios with two-member teams made up of university faculty, principals, teachers, curriculum leaders, counselors, and superintendents.

In a pilot study conducted in District #21 in Wheeling, Illinois, student teachers enrolled in the Professional Development School in conjunction with Illinois State University spent an entire year working in the classroom with mentor teachers. As part of the partnership, the student teachers were required to keep portfolios that included their philosophy of teaching, their credentials, units they created, artifacts from students, and evidence showing that they could transfer ideas learned in college classes to the elementary and middle school students they taught.

Career portfolios enable professional educators to collect and organize artifacts that showcase their experience and qualifications.

Career Portfolio

"A teaching portfolio should be more than a miscellaneous collection of artifacts or an extended list of professional activities. It should carefully and thoughtfully document a set of accomplishments attained over an extended period." (Wolf 1996, 34)

Career portfolios enable professional educators to collect and organize artifacts that showcase their experience and qualifications. These portfolios are used for job interviews and promotions. They can be very effective if they include reflections or insights on teaching as well as connections of the entries to school-wide goals, standards, or expectations. Wolf has suggested several ways to organize a career portfolio. One organizational plan includes the following:

Contents

    I. Background information

        A. Updated résumé

        B. Transcript of course work

        C. Philosophy of teaching

        D. Teaching goals

        E. People who have influenced me

II. Teaching artifacts
   A. Videotape of teaching
   B. Unit plans
   C. Lesson plans
   D. Student work samples
   E. Reflections on artifacts
   F. Assessments
   G. Pictures of group projects
   H. Videotapes of student performances

III. School involvement
   A. Committee work
   B. Extracurricular sponsorships
   C. Letters to students, parents
   D. Letters from students, parents

IV. Professional information
   A. Memberships in professional organizations
   B. Letters of recommendation
   C. Letters of commendation
   D. Formal evaluations
   E. Awards, certificates

(Adapted from Wolf 1996, 35. Reprinted with permission.)

Many educators have found the compilation of a career portfolio to be a project they recommend for others—especially if they are requiring students to create portfolios.

An action research portfolio provides the organizational framework for collecting and reflecting on the data throughout the entire process and documents the evidence.

Action Research Portfolios

"Action research has been defined as 'research carried out by practitioners with a view to improving their professional practice and understanding it better.'" (Cameron-Jones 1983, as cited by Borg et al. 1993, 390)

Action research enables professionals to reflect on whether they can perform better. An individual or a cadre using action research can identify problem areas and seek methods to correct them. Inquiry, reflection, collaboration, and continual self-improvement are aspects of action research that professionals can use to expand their knowledge base, their repertoire of strategies, and their team-building skills.

Teachers enrolled in the Field-Based Master's Program sponsored by Saint Xavier University and IRI/SkyLight Training and Publishing in Illinois work individually or in teams to define a problem, establish data collection processes, identify probable causes of the problem, design and use intervention strategies to reduce the problem as defined, evaluate the effectiveness of the interventions, and make recommendations for future study. An action research portfolio provides the organizational framework for collecting and reflecting on the data throughout the entire process and documenting the evidence.

Professional Development Portfolios

This book describes many options educators can explore to become reflective practitioners, but the focus will be on developing professional development plans and professional portfolios. This dual focus will enable educators to

1. Articulate their visions of teaching and learning

2. Develop professional goals

3. Select learner-centered goals

4. Document progress in achieving the goals

5. Interact with peers throughout the entire process

6. Reflect on the learning experience and attainment of goals

7. Share insights with others in conferences

The Informal Track

Many educators develop professional portfolios as part of their professional development plans or as an alternative to attending inservice meetings. Educators work toward their goals and document their progress in portfolios they later share with colleagues and supervisors. This informal process does not require official documentation, monitoring, or review. It is simply another method whereby educators can expand their repertoire of teaching tools, grow as professionals, and meet with colleagues to discuss ideas and concerns.

The Formal Track

Some schools and districts are using professional development plans and portfolios in their official performance review process. Instead of being an option, the portfolio is required as part of a summative evaluation of an educator's performance. The requirements for the formal portfolio are more structured and usually include measurable goals: baseline data (a description of students' achievement at the beginning of the intervention); specific methods of data collection; methods of assessment; observations by peers, mentors, and supervisors; conferences with a supervisor; and a final evaluation scoring guide. Chapter 8 describes the evaluation process and the importance of providing clear guidelines and criteria for evaluation if the professional development portfolio is to become part of an educator's official evaluation. Ideas discussed throughout the book can be used for both informal and formal tracks; however, criteria that are critical to a formal portfolio will be indicated.

Many educators develop professional portfolios as part of their professional growth plan or as an alternative to attending inservice meetings.

IRI/SkyLight Training and Publishing, Inc.

The Standards Track

Various agencies have developed standards for teacher certification. Teachers usually demonstrate their attainment of these standards through performance-based assessments and portfolios that include videotapes of classroom interactions, an analysis of strategies used to promote students' learnings, and reflective commentaries in which teachers "think about their instructional practices and evaluate their effectiveness" (Buday and Kelley 1996, 216). Chapter 8 will describe some of the standards that have been proposed.

The professional development portfolio as delineated in the next nine chapters describes the ideas, options, and formats educators can explore in their pursuit of professional growth.

The Journey

The journey to professional development is rewarding when one is accompanied by a travel companion to share reactions, reflections, and insights. It is highly recommended that each professional join with one or two colleagues either to address similar professional goals or to exchange ideas about progress in achieving different goals.

Kathy Brown's Journey

To personalize the professional portfolio process, many of the examples will focus on a fictitious eleventh-grade English teacher, Kathy Brown. Kathy will go through all the steps in the book, and readers will get a chance to "get inside her head" as they read her reflections and see her artifacts.

Sometimes the parts of a portfolio appear fragmented when introduced separately; therefore, the Appendix contains Kathy's completed professional portfolio. Notice how Kathy does not embark on her professional journey alone. She has several peers, mentors, and supervisors who are helping her accomplish her goals along the way.

Each chapter includes the following:

1. A research review
2. A description of the process
3. Four examples of portfolio entries
4. Blackline masters of some of the examples
5. A reflections page to record thoughts and reactions

Join Kathy as she begins the process of designing her professional portfolio for change.

The journey to professional development is rewarding when one is accompanied by a travel companion to share reactions, reflections, and insights.

Chapter 1

Philosophy of Professional Growth for Teachers

"The development of professional skills and knowledge should span the entire career. Those who stop growing after receiving tenure or upon approaching retirement hurt themselves and those they teach and supervise." (Glatthorn 1996, 46)

Professional Status

"Professionalism is a form of liberty that is not simply conferred; it is earned." (Delaney and Sykes, in Lieberman 1988, 3)

Teachers want to be valued and treated as professionals and gain the respect of the public in order to make autonomous decisions to help the students they teach. Delaney and Sykes (as cited in Lieberman 1988, 3) say the question of whether teachers should gain the status of "professionalism" has already been settled by many— "of course we must have teachers who are thoroughly schooled and helpfully inducted, who are autonomous and responsible, who are valued and treated as professionals!" They note, however, that "this view is not self-evident to all who participate in or observe teachers' work. If entertained at all, it is not clearly and firmly settled in the minds of citizens, law makers, bureaucrats, school board members, district administrators, school principals, or even all teachers."

Darling-Hammond (as cited in Lieberman 1988) argues that if teachers want to make decisions without external regulations, they must adhere to at least three prerequisites to professional claims for self-governance:

1. Knowledge of the principles, theories, and factors that undergird appropriate decisions about what procedures should be employed— and knowledge of the procedures themselves.

2. The ability to apply this knowledge in nonroutine circumstances, taking relevant considerations into account.

3. A commitment to do what is best for the client, not what is easiest or most expedient.

Definitions of Teaching

Eisner discusses two meanings of the word "teaching." Teaching can be regarded as a "set of acts performed by people we call teachers as they attempt to foster learning" (Eisner 1985, 180). By this definition, when teachers engage in activities such as lecturing, asking questions, leading discussions, or demonstrating ideas, they are teaching.

Eisner also describes the view espoused by John Dewey, who felt that the term *teaching* was similar to the term *selling*. "That is, one could not teach unless someone learned, just as one could not sell unless someone bought. Teaching and learning were regarded as reciprocal concepts. . . . Thus, if a teacher attempts to teach but does not succeed in helping the students learn, then he or she may be said to have lectured, conducted a discussion, demonstrated, explained but *not* to have taught. To teach, in this sense, is known by its effects" (Eisner 1985, 179).

Before educators begin the professional development process, then, they need to ask themselves some important questions about teaching:

1. What is my role as a teacher?
2. How can I best meet the needs of my students?
3. What methodologies are most effective?
4. Can I vary my instructional strategies to help my special needs students?
5. How much content or basic skills is enough? How much is too much?
6. How can I be a more effective teacher?

Before educators begin the professional development process, they need to ask themselves some important questions about teaching.

Theories of Learning

Before educators can plan their own professional development, they also need to clarify their roles as teachers and how they view the learning process. Some educators, reflecting on their own learning experiences, might feel that "skill and drill" exercises and memorization were and still are fundamental to learning. Others may feel that instead of the "pour and store" philosophy of attaining knowledge, students learn best when they construct their own understanding of the world. According to this latter view, students make sense of the world by integrating new experiences into what they already know and understand. Teachers holding this view would agree with Brooks and Brooks (1993, 5) that "educators must invite students to experience the world's richness, empower them to ask their own questions and seek their own answers, and challenge them to understand the world's complexities."

Other educators might follow Feuerstein's concept of mediated learning. Mediated learning occurs when teachers help learners "frame, filter, and schedule stimuli" that ultimately influence how the students transfer knowledge. "Mediation assumes that instruction is more concerned with *going beyond* the information given, with connecting the present with both the past and the anticipation of the future, than with mastering specific bits of here-and-now data" (Presseisen and Kozulin 1992, as cited in Ben-Hur 1994, 57). It is essential, therefore, that teachers form opinions and theories about how students learn before they develop their personal philosophies, pose essential questions, or set professional goals.

Before educators develop professional goals, they need to ask themselves how they feel about learning:

1. How do I learn best?

2. How do students learn best?

3. Can all students learn?

4. What can I do to mediate students' learning?

5. Which learning theories seem most effective for my students?

Purpose for Professional Portfolios

Educators about to embark on a professional enrichment journey, with the goal of helping their students learn, need first to reflect on their purpose for developing a professional portfolio. Dietz (1995, 41) recommends that participants begin the process by clarifying their purposes for the portfolio and formulating their *credo*—their basic values and belief systems that drive their decisions and learning as teachers." Writing a "philosophy of education" is usually required for applications to graduate schools and for some job applications, but veteran teachers rarely take time to think about teaching and learning. More importantly, they seldom reflect on how their philosophy shapes their attitudes and performance. When asked what evidence or artifact in her portfolio best showed her growth and development as a professional, one student teacher enrolled in a professional development school, responded, "My philosophy of teaching, because before I wrote it, I had to really think about what I believe in about teaching. That's really the first step to becoming the kind of teacher I want to be."

Ownership of Professional Development

Educators also need to ask themselves if they are ready and willing to assume the autonomy and the responsibility of professionalism by assessing their needs, setting their goals, reflecting on their practices, and changing their practices to better meet the needs of students.

Educators must then continue to ask themselves key questions along the way: Who is ultimately responsible for my growth as a professional?

It is essential that teachers form opinions and theories about how students learn before they develop their personal philosophies or set professional goals.

What are my goals? What will I have to do to meet those goals? How will I measure my success?

Bernhardt (1994, 138) states, "A school culture ready for improvement consists of colleagues able to share their personal values, beliefs, and visions; able to communicate and collaborate with one another to build and implement a shared vision and mission; and able to trust each other to behave in a manner consistent with a new school mission and vision."

Covey (as cited in Bernhardt 1994, 138) believes that four basic needs must be recognized before individuals in an organization are willing to share a vision and collaborate: (1) the need for human growth and development; (2) the need to be treated well; (2) the need to contribute and have meaning; and (4) the need to be treated fairly. These needs must be met in professional development training because educators must believe that the investment they make in establishing goals and documenting their experience in portfolios will increase their students' overall performance.

The reculturing of the school will not be successful if only some of the educators assume responsibility for their professional development.

The reculturing of the school will not be successful if only some of the educators assume responsibility for their professional development, while others welcome the demise of staff development days but neglect to embark on the journey to "earn" their professionalism. Darling-Hammond (1996, 10) warns that "major changes in the productivity of American schools rest on our ability to create and sustain a highly prepared teaching force for all, not just some, of our children." Similarly, the opportunity for educators to take charge of professional development must be explored by all, not just some, of our teachers.

The Power of Peer Interaction

Before educators can decide upon the course of professional development, they need to review their beliefs about teaching, learning, and professional development. Sharing ideas with peers helps clarify thinking processes; therefore, it is beneficial to include a friend, colleague, or mentor on the journey with whom to share ideas and encouragement. Working in cadres allows professionals to form a community of lifelong learners and to demonstrate to all concerned parties that "professionalism is a form of liberty that is not simply conferred; it is earned" (Delaney and Sykes, in Lieberman 1988, 3).

Kathy's Journey

Dietz (1995) recommends that educators first clarify the basic values and belief systems that drive their decisions about teaching and learning. Teachers often reflect on their positive and negative teaching and learning experiences, formulate their own vision of teaching and learning, and develop or re-examine their philosophy of teaching and learning before they develop a professional development plan. The following examples show how Kathy Brown, the fictitious teacher whose journey is being documented, started the process.

IRI/SkyLight Training and Publishing, Inc.

Examples

Reflections on My Learning Experiences

Share your responses with a peer.

1. Describe how your favorite teacher influenced your teaching.

   One teacher read every Friday with the whole class for one hour. I usually finished the book over the weekend. I became a lifelong reader because of her.

2. Describe a positive or negative incident that has affected you.

   When I was in an algebra class, our teacher used the scores on a test to seat us—highest to lowest scores. I have never been so embarrassed and I grew to hate algebra.

   Kathy Brown
   August 26

Reflections on My Teaching Experiences

Share your responses with a peer.

1. Explain your greatest success as an educator.

   I've succeeded when students are reading other novels by the authors we have studied.

2. Explain your greatest challenge as an educator.

   Grading the performances of students quickly, fairly, and meaningfully. I hate the grading process.

   Kathy Brown
   August 26

My Vision of Teaching and Learning

Share your responses with a peer.

1. To create the "School of Best Practices," I would choose:
   - *Cooperative learning*
   - *Team building*
   - *Block Scheduling*
   - *Integrated curricula*
   - *Authentic assessment*

2. What topics or problems in education would you like to explore to help your students?

   To know more about rubrics or scoring guides to help students assess their own work.

   Kathy Brown
   August 26

My Philosophy of Teaching and Learning

I believe that good teachers provide the framework for student learning. That framework includes:

1. *A warm and caring classroom*
2. *A knowledge base*
3. *Opportunities for meaningful interaction with the content and their peers*
4. *A fair and effective assessment process*

I believe students will learn best if I mediate their learning and then let them "fly on their own."

Signed: *Kathy Brown*   Date: *8/22*

Peer signature: *Patsy Angel*   Date: *8/28*

Reflections on My Learning Experiences

Share your responses with a peer.

1. Describe how your favorite teacher influenced your teaching.

2. Describe a positive or negative incident that has affected you.

Signed: _____ Date:_____

Reflections on My Teaching Experiences

Share your responses with a peer.

1. Explain your greatest success as an educator.

2. Explain your greatest challenge as an educator.

Signed: _____ Date:_____

Peer: _____ Date:_____

My Vision of Teaching and Learning

Share your responses with a peer.

1. To create the "School of Best Practices," I would include the following teaching and learning experiences:

2. To help my students, I would like to explore these topics:

Signed: _____ Date:_____

My Philosophy of Teaching and Learning

Signed: _____ Date: _____

Peer: _____ Date: _____

The Professional Development Process

"To be successful, restructuring must start with a few clear goals to be achieved. Clear goals do not ensure success because a lot can happen along the way, but without them, it seems unlikely that a school or district will emerge from the process [to school improvement] triumphantly." (Ellis and Fouts 1994, 27)

School Improvement

Classical Research Approach

The so-called "classical research approach" to school improvement depends on the universities to provide the research-based knowledge that is passed on for teachers to use with students. This research is passed on through college coursework, journals, conferences, and inservices. The research is often based on cause-and-effect relationships, with variables and data describing populations totally different from the teachers who are expected to apply the research in their classrooms. "This classical approach has been largely from the top down" (Eisner 1991, 11). Moreover, if teachers do refer to or use traditional research in their classes, it is usually because they are taking courses in a degree program that requires them to do so. Once the course or program is finished, they seldom read or use research again.

Action Research Approach

Educators value research that is practical and applicable to their students. Scientific researchers look at what others are doing, whereas action researchers reflect on their own practice and then seek creative ways to improve their practice. Eisner (1991, 6) says that such "inquiry" methods can reveal the qualities of classrooms and schools and the processes of teaching—"teaching is a form of qualitative inquiry."

Who knows better than the classroom teacher what specific problems he is having with curriculum coverage, classroom management, student motivation, or student achievement? Who knows better than the classroom teacher what types of new teaching strategies might work with his students? What about Gardner's theories of multiple intelligences? What if I use portfolios to measure growth and development for my grouped class? These are questions and areas the individual teacher, a group of teachers, or a faculty could address through informal qualitative research. Harp (1994) says that the role of teacher as a researcher has been an "untapped" source of acquiring important information about both the teaching process and the learning process.

Patterson, Stansell, and Lee (1990, vii) have described the untapped power of teacher research as follows:

> Teachers can move beyond kidwatching to do systematic research in their classrooms. We argue that teachers' research can inform specific instructional decisions, but we also explore the potential for these research findings to influence teachers' personal theories and our collective theoretical understandings. Teacher research promises to offer teachers a tool for professional development and a vehicle for gaining power in the profession and in policy-making arenas.

"All persons have the potential to grow, to change, to develop. The ultimate goal is self-directed professionals who can direct, manage, and evaluate their own professional development." (Glatthorn 1996, 46)

The Team Approach

"Teachers, like other professionals, perform more effectively—even exponentially—if they collaborate. Although collaboration represents a significant change in how most teachers work, it should become an expectation." (Schmoker 1996, 7)

Some of the most effective professional development is the result of cadres of teachers working together, making decisions, analyzing and using data, planning curricula, monitoring student achievement, and evaluating the effectiveness of the new approaches (Bernhardt 1994). Teachers used to working in the "hermetically sealed classroom" often welcome the support from colleagues and will work together to achieve a common goal.

One starting point could be to have interested teachers meet weekly to discuss books or articles read in advance. Hoerr (1996, 381) feels that "discussing such readings is a good way to begin talking about significant issues in a collegial setting."

McGreal says that the next generation of professional development plans will come from schools where many things are done in teams. The same teams that are already established—grade-level teams, interdisciplinary teams, interdepartmental teams—decide to develop a professional

Teachers used to working in the "hermetically sealed classroom" often welcome the support from colleagues and will work together to achieve a common goal.

development plan for the team. The administrator can meet with team members once or twice a year for progress reports and assist them in collecting data, providing resources, and securing substitutes so members can visit other classes or schools. The teachers can write a curriculum, present workshops, develop an ungraded classroom program, or create peer coaching teams. As McGreal (as cited in Brandt 1996, 32) explains, "They can do action research projects or curriculum development. They might develop a workshop for other teachers. And when they've done it, they meet again and plan something different—so everybody is involved in a professional development plan all the time."

Groups of teachers engaged in problem solving create a strong sense of group purpose. This environment enhances professional satisfaction and "encourages teachers to reflect on their practice and explore ways to improve it on an ongoing, rather than episodic basis. It is an environment in which it is safe to be candid and to take the risks inherent in trying out new ideas or unfamiliar practices" (McLaughlin and Yee, in Lieberman 1988, 36). The team approach to professional development also allows more opportunities for study groups and peer coaching, whereby members can observe each other, give feedback, cover classes, discuss new ideas, implement innovative strategies, and evaluate the effectiveness of their plan and their own growth and development.

The Flow of Professional Growth

Once an approach to school improvement is chosen, educators will sometimes know exactly what topic they want to investigate. At other times, they are not sure what areas they would like to explore in depth. They need to discuss topics with others in order to decide. Sometimes entire faculties meet at the beginning of the school year and break into small groups to discuss common goals. The flow chart suggests one method to move from the selection of a topic to the development of a professional development plan.

The team approach to professional development also allows more opportunities for study groups and peer coaching.

Flow Chart of Professional Growth

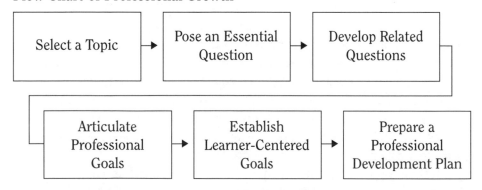

Select a Topic → Pose an Essential Question → Develop Related Questions → Articulate Professional Goals → Establish Learner-Centered Goals → Prepare a Professional Development Plan

Select a Topic

Figure 2.1 (page 24) provides a list of professional development topics that educators might want to explore in depth to decide how implementation of these ideas or strategies could help the students. Educators should review the topics and decide upon the areas that meet the needs of their students or their school.

Pose an Essential Question

Often the discussions about various topics help educators explore options and examine possibilities in depth. Sometimes the terms may be new to the group; at other times, people have heard the terms but are not sure what they really mean. Eisner (1985) believes that focusing on educational theories helps educators focus attention on some aspects of the classroom they might otherwise neglect.

One way to narrow the topic and make it more manageable for a one- to two-year commitment is to pose an essential question. The essential question should ask how studying and implementing the idea would help the students, the teachers, the administrators, the school, or the district. This essential question would then drive the professional development plan.

Figure 2.2 (page 25) provides examples of how educators at the elementary, middle school, and high school levels can select a topic and develop an essential question to help develop goals.

Develop Related Questions

Once educators have identified the essential research question individually, as a small group, or as an entire faculty, it is important to develop a series of related research questions (see Figure 2.3, page 26). These questions are similar to what Dietz calls "splinter questions" because they dig deeper and cover other aspects or "subpoints" of the essential research question.

Articulate Professional Goals

Psychologist Mihalyi Csikszentmihalyi (1990) talks about the enjoyment people get from pursuing doable goals that they value. This connection of goals to happiness accounts for many people being as happy or happier at work than at leisure. Schmoker (1996, 18) says goals drive us—"unfortunately, most schools do not make the connection between goals, motivation, and improvement . . . without explicit learning goals, we are simply not set up and organized for improvement, for results. Only such goals will allow us to analyze, monitor, and adjust practice towards improvement."

Educators need to articulate professional goals and learn more about a topic in order to set learner-centered goals for their students. Educators need to set specific goals and know their audience—in other words, who will benefit from the implementation of this plan? Feuerstein's theory of Mediated Learning Experience considers the importance of knowing not

Once educators have identified the essential research question, it is important to develop a series of related research questions.

Professional Development Topics

From the following topics, check two items in each category that you want to explore in depth. Talk to colleagues about how these topics or strategies could help the students.

Structural Formats

- ☐ Multiage Classroom
- ☐ Detracking
- ☐ Block Scheduling
- ☐ Year-Round School
- ☐ Team Teaching
- ☐ Grouping Practices
- ☐ Inclusion
- ☐ _____
- ☐ _____

Instructional Innovation

- ☐ Instructional Strategies
- ☐ Classroom Management
- ☐ Cooperative Learning Strategies
- ☐ Multiple Intelligences Theory
- ☐ Graphic Organizers
- ☐ Higher-Order Thinking Skills
- ☐ Technology
- ☐ Metacognition
- ☐ Transfer
- ☐ Teacher Expectation and Student Achievement (TESA)
- ☐ Mediated Learning
- ☐ _____
- ☐ _____

Curricular Possibilities

- ☐ Standards Development
- ☐ Thematic Teaching
- ☐ Curriculum Integration
- ☐ Case Studies
- ☐ Service Learning Projects
- ☐ Experiential Education
- ☐ Mentorship-Apprenticeship
- ☐ Problem-Based Learning
- ☐ Project-Based Learning

- ☐ School-to-Work Transition
- ☐ Performance Learning
- ☐ Curriculum Development
- ☐ Expeditionary Learning
- ☐ _____
- ☐ _____

Collegial Strategies

- ☐ Team Building
- ☐ Consensus Building
- ☐ Strategic Planning
- ☐ Team Teaching
- ☐ Curriculum Mapping
- ☐ Conflict Resolution
- ☐ Peer Mediation
- ☐ Parent Councils
- ☐ Peer Coaching
- ☐ Mentoring
- ☐ Action Research Teams
- ☐ Working with the Community
- ☐ _____
- ☐ _____

Evaluation Techniques

- ☐ Assessment of Standards
- ☐ Student Portfolios
- ☐ Teacher-Made Tests
- ☐ Authentic Performances
- ☐ Project Evaluations
- ☐ Standardized Tests
- ☐ Performance Rubrics
- ☐ Individual Evaluation Plans
- ☐ Professional Portfolios
- ☐ Report Card Revisions
- ☐ Communicating Results to Parents
- ☐ _____
- ☐ _____

Figure 2.1

Educators decide which topics to implement.

IRI/SkyLight Training and Publishing, Inc.

Posing an Essential Question

ELEMENTARY SCHOOL LEVEL

Curriculum Revisions

How do we combine our whole-language and phonics programs to meet students' needs?

Multiple Intelligences

Will students' motivation improve if we plan lessons using Gardner's Multiple Intelligences theory?

Classroom Management

Do we continue to reward good behavior or do we encourage high expectations to motivate learning?

Cooperative Learning Strategies

Would students' behavior problems decrease if teachers taught social skills explicitly?

MIDDLE SCHOOL LEVEL

Problem-Based Learning

Would students' test scores improve if we adopted problem-based learning in science courses?

Curriculum Integration and Project Evaluation

How would we grade performances for integrated units?

Team Teaching

Would team teaching be more effective if team members engaged in team-building strategies with their group and students?

Peer Mediation

Would peer mediation reduce student conflicts and help them manage their emotions?

SECONDARY SCHOOL LEVEL

Year-Round School

Would student achievement increase in year-round schools?

Metacognition

Would students acquire independent problem-solving skills if required to reflect metacognitively on projects and performances?

Block Scheduling

Would block scheduling affect student achievement and motivation?

Standardized Tests

What would happen to students' ACT and SAT test scores if we included a two-week review in every course prior to the tests?

Figure 2.2

Posing essential questions helps educators develop goals.

IRI/SkyLight Training and Publishing, Inc.

Developing Related Research Questions

QUESTION FOR AN INDIVIDUAL

Topic: Standardized Tests

Essential Research Question: Will my students score higher on standardized tests if I teach explicit thinking skills?

Related Questions:

1. *Should I teach thinking skills separately from or integrated with content?*
2. *Should I focus on two or three thinking skills or teach them all?*
3. *Should I use graphic organizers to teach each thinking skill?*
4. *Should I teach thinking skills using one system or a variety of systems? Which are the best ones?*
5. *How should I assess student progress?*

QUESTION FOR A GROUP

Topic: Assessment of Standards

Essential Research Question: How can fourth-grade teachers assess the range of ability levels of students?

Related Questions:

1. *How can we help special needs students meet the standards?*
2. *Will portfolios prove that students meet or do not meet standards?*
3. *Can fourth-grade students construct rubrics for each standard?*
4. *Can teachers construct rubrics to measure the standards consistently?*
5. *What happens when students do not meet the standards?*

QUESTION FOR THE SCHOOL

Topic: Block Scheduling

Essential Research Question: How will block scheduling help our students?

Related Questions:

1. *What are block scheduling options?*
2. *What training do we need?*
3. *Will student achievement increase?*
4. *What happens when courses don't convene every day?*
5. *What does the research say about the effects of block scheduling?*

Figure 2.3

Developing related questions sharpens the focus of essential research.

only the *what* and *how* of our goals but also the *why*. The results should transcend a particular learning activity or goal and lead to true meaning for the educator and for students.

"Even when schools establish goals, the goals tend to be too general. This unfortunate case of 'general goals' creates a sense of 'false clarity'—the erroneous belief that we understand and know how to work towards achieving the goals." (Fullan 1991, 34–35)

Establishing specific goals are crucial to improvement:

- Specific goals convey a message directly to teachers that they are capable of improvement.

- Specific goals provide a basis for rational decision making, for ways to organize and execute instruction.

- Specific goals enable teachers to gauge their success.

- Specific goals promote professional dialogue.

(Rosenholtz 1989, as cited in Schmoker 1996, 23)

Establish Learner-Centered Goals

Glickman (as cited in Schmoker 1996) differentiates "innovations," which he criticizes, and objectives, which he advocates. The major difference between the two is that innovations like technology, cooperative learning, whole-language instruction, or interdisciplinary instruction can be considered successful by faculty members by the very fact that they are *implemented*. The results, however, should not be measured by the successful implementation of an innovation but by *whether students learned*. Glickman believes that the "litmus test for a good school is not its innovations but rather the solid, purposeful, enduring results it tries to obtain for its students" (Glickman 1993, 50). When a faculty states that its goal is "to show that our school can move into the twenty-first century through technology" (48), it puts emphasis on what the *teachers will do* rather than what the *students will learn*. Schmoker (1996, 25) uses a table (see Figure 2.4) to illustrate Glickman's comparison of innovations and objectives (goals).

Innovations can be considered successful by the very fact that they are implemented. The results, however, should not be measured by the successful implementation but by whether students learned.

Innovations Compared to Objectives

Innovation	Objective
Technology	Students will learn how to use various forms of technology to improve their performance.
Cooperative Learning	Students will learn how to operate in groups, and their achievements and attitudes will reflect the skills learned.
Whole-Language Instruction	Students will acquire a more positive attitude toward reading, read with more comprehension, and write more creatively and analytically.
Interdisciplinary Instruction	Students will be better able to solve problems by drawing from various disciplines.

(Schmoker 1996, 25. Reprinted with permission.) **Figure 2.4**

It is important, therefore, that educators look closely at their research questions and make sure the essential question and the related questions ask how the students will benefit. Even if the question relates to something structural like block scheduling, educators must not ask how the school or the teachers will benefit but how the students will gain from switching from traditional 50-minute periods to 70–90 minute blocks of time.

It is important that educators look closely at their research questions and make sure the essential question and the related questions ask how the students will benefit.

Developing Learner-Centered Goals

Essential Questions	Learner-Centered Goals
Would students' behavioral problems decrease if each teacher taught social skills explicitly?	Students will learn to: • listen to each other • share ideas • encourage each other • disagree with ideas—not people • reach consensus
Would students' test scores improve if we used problem-based learning in our science courses?	Students will learn to: • reason analytically • solve problems independently • solve problems collaboratively • apply problem-solving techniques to science experiments
Would block scheduling change the way students learn?	Students will learn to: • work cooperatively to create projects • construct knowledge for themselves • reflect metacognitively on their learning • produce quality performances • understand key concepts of learning
Would portfolios show growth and development for gifted and special needs students?	Students will learn to: • collect key samples of their work • reflect on their learning • select examples that show growth • discuss what they have learned • demonstrate their growth and development

Figure 2.5

IRI/SkyLight Training and Publishing, Inc.

". . . the last ten years should have taught us that establishing vague process or procedural goals in the absence of clear, concrete learning goals is foolish. Each undergirds the other. Learning goals give meaning to and act as a healthy check on the traditionally untethered tendency for public institutions to be satisfied with processes, regardless of outcomes." (Schmoker 1996, 27)

The next logical step in the professional development process is to establish the specific learner goals that the person developing the plan hopes to achieve. The steps in developing learner-centered goals could be organized in many ways. The example in Figure 2.6 shows how one team of teachers progressed from selecting a topic to formulating an essential question they wanted to investigate. The team brainstormed related questions that could also be addressed and then developed specific learner-centered goals to drive their research and provide the framework for their professional development plan and their portfolios.

Learning goals give meaning to and act as a healthy check on the traditionally untethered tendency for public institutions to be satisfied with processes, regardless of outcomes.

Goal Development Process

Name: _Patsy Saunders, Jim Smith, Frank Baker_   Date: _8/97_

Topic: _Classroom Management_

Essential Question:

Would students' behavior problems decrease if each teacher taught social skills explicitly during the year?

Related Questions:

1. *How much time should be spent teaching the social skills?*
2. *What specific strategies should be used to teach the skills?*
3. *Should students' social skills be assessed?*
4. *How will we know our interventions worked?*
5. *Will social skills transfer outside the classrooms?*

Professional Goals:

To research information on classroom management and to talk to teachers who have mastered classroom management.

Goals:

As a result of teaching social skills explicitly, the students will:

1. *reduce the number of behavior problems*
2. *listen to each other*
3. *respect ideas of others*
4. *share materials and workloads*
5. *encourage and help each other*
6. *disagree with the idea, not the person*

Figure 2.6

Prepare a Professional Development Plan

After educators have developed their learner goals, they often begin a professional development plan that helps them focus on what they need to do to meet their goals. These plans vary from school to school and district to district, but the following items could be included:

Professional Development Plan Options

- ☐ Name
- ☐ Proposed Timeframe
- ☐ Topic of Interest or Concern
- ☐ Essential Question
- ☐ Related Questions
- ☐ Professional Goals
- ☐ Learner-Centered Goals
- ☐ Action Plan (Activities, Interventions, Timelines)
- ☐ Resources (Books, Videos, People)

- ☐ Team Members Involved
- ☐ Observations Planned
- ☐ Baseline Data (Diagnostic Information)
- ☐ Documentation for Portfolio
- ☐ Ways to Assess Effectiveness
- ☐ Checkpoints
- ☐ Conference Options
- ☐ Evaluation Options (Formal Performance Review)

Figure 2.7

It is important that educators include some baseline data to show the status of students before the intervention is introduced.

Informal Track

Educators on the informal track for professional development can decide what items they want to include in their professional development plan and, in most cases, in their portfolios. They may want to share their plans with peers and supervisors, but since they are conducting their own professional development, they have many options. Usually, however, they do fill out a one- or two-page plan stating their goals and how they plan to achieve them.

Formal Track

Educators may be required to develop an official professional development plan to share with a supervisor as part of their yearly staff development or their performance review. Many teachers include this plan in their professional portfolio and in their personnel file. The formal plan usually contains the items cited in Figure 2.7. It is important that educators include some baseline or diagnostic data to show the status of students *before* the intervention or action plan is introduced. In addition, educators should mention how they plan to evaluate the effectiveness of their intervention and the attainment of their goal. Also, the summative professional development plan will usually contain formal checkpoints that include observations and conferences with a supervisor. The plan will culminate in a final portfolio conference and formal evaluation of the professional portfolio.

In other words, the formal track is more standardized, with specific items for inclusion and clear criteria for evaluating the professional development plan and the portfolio. Often, the format for the plans will have been developed by the school or district. Other times, educators can develop their own plan incorporating specific items relevant to their goals.

Figure 2.8 shows the major differences between the process and products of the informal track and the formal track.

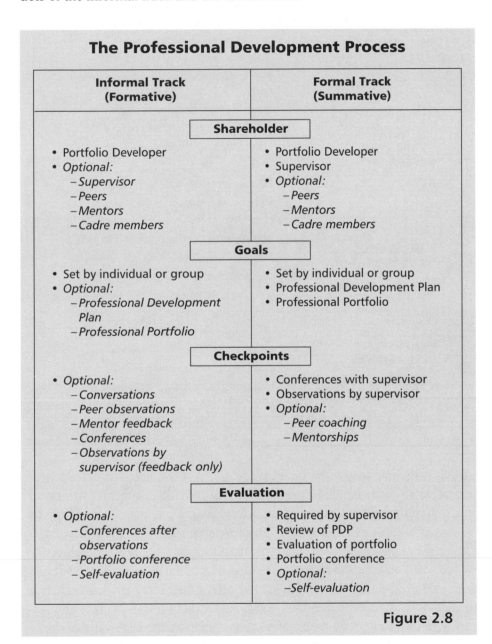

The Professional Development Process

Informal Track (Formative)	Formal Track (Summative)
Shareholder	

• Portfolio Developer
• *Optional:*
  – *Supervisor*
  – *Peers*
  – *Mentors*
  – *Cadre members*
	• Portfolio Developer
	• Supervisor
	• *Optional:*
	  – *Peers*
	  – *Mentors*
	  – *Cadre members*

Goals	

• Set by individual or group
• *Optional:*
  – *Professional Development Plan*
  – *Professional Portfolio*
	• Set by individual or group
	• Professional Development Plan
	• Professional Portfolio

Checkpoints	

• *Optional:*
  – *Conversations*
  – *Peer observations*
  – *Mentor feedback*
  – *Conferences*
  – *Observations by supervisor (feedback only)*
	• Conferences with supervisor
	• Observations by supervisor
	• *Optional:*
	  – *Peer coaching*
	  – *Mentorships*

Evaluation	

• *Optional:*
  – *Conferences after observations*
  – *Portfolio conference*
  – *Self-evaluation*
	• Required by supervisor
	• Review of PDP
	• Evaluation of portfolio
	• Portfolio conference
	• *Optional:*
	  – *Self-evaluation*

Figure 2.8

Professional Development Timelines

Allowing educators to direct their own professional development allows for flexibility in scheduling and timelines. Most people prefer to set their own timelines depending upon their purpose and their individual goals. The timeline in Figure 2.9 (page 32) helps explain the essential steps and provides some suggested dates.

Timeline for Professional Development

PHASE ONE: **CHALLENGE** **OR PROBLEM** *Date: Aug.–Sept.*	• Select a topic • Pose an essential question • Develop related questions • Articulate professional goals • Establish learner-centered goals • Prepare a professional development plan
PHASE TWO: **RESEARCH** *Date: Oct.–Nov.*	• Review research on the topic • Locate available resources • Collect baseline data • Decide on needed documentation • Determine evaluation methods
PHASE THREE: **IMPLEMENTATION** *Date: Nov.–March*	• Collect data (artifacts, videos, surveys) • Meet with peers to discuss progress • Observe and be observed • Monitor progress toward goals
PHASE FOUR: **CULMINATION** *Date: March–June*	• Select items for final portfolios • Reflect on progress and products • Organize professional portfolio • Share professional development plan and portfolio

Figure 2.9

Many people need time to research available resources and learn more about a topic before they can establish baseline data, data collection, evaluation methods, or timelines.

This timeline may have to be adapted to meet the needs of individual educators or entire faculties. Sometimes it is difficult to submit a professional development plan early in the school year. Many people need time to research available resources and learn more about a topic before they can establish baseline data, data collection, evaluation methods, or timelines.

One option includes submitting the professional development plan two or three months after the start of school, after educators have had a chance to acquaint themselves with their topic. A second option includes submitting a preliminary professional development plan at the beginning of the school year and then revising or updating the plan after a period of study and planning. Often the timeline for submitting the plan is flexible, depending on the familiarity of educators with their topic.

IRI/SkyLight Training and Publishing, Inc.

Examples

Developing Research Questions

Name: *Kathy Brown*   Date: *August*

Topic: *Performance Rubrics*

Essential Question:
Can students develop rubrics to evaluate their work?

Related Questions:

1. *Will rubrics promote consistency in grading?*

2. *Will students generate criteria to evaluate their work?*

3. *How does traditional grading compare to rubrics?*

4. *Will students' work improve?*

5. *Will students evaluate their own work?*

Developing Learner-Centered Goals

Name: *Kathy Brown*   Date: *August*

Essential Question:
Can students develop rubrics to evaluate their work?

Professional Goals

1. *Review research on performance assessment*
2. *Attend workshops and conferences*
3. *Visit teachers and schools using rubrics*

Learner-Centered Goals

As a result of introducing performance rubrics, students will:
1. *Determine criteria for all work*
2. *Create indicators of quality work*
3. *Develop rubrics to evaluate their work*

Professional Development Plan (Part One)

Name: *Kathy Brown*   Date: *August*

Topic selected: *Performance Rubrics*

Baseline Data:
Before using rubrics, I will ask students to evaluate one paper they wrote and one speech they gave (on video). I will collect the grades they give themselves and the grades I give them.

Action Plan (Intervention):
I will teach students how to create assessment criteria and indicators. We will create scoring rubrics for assessing their written and oral work.

Timeline:
September–April

Professional Development Plan (Part Two)

Name: *Kathy Brown*   Date: *September*

Topic selected: *Performance Rubrics*

Documentation of Study:
I plan to collect:

1. *Copies of students' self-evaluations done without rubrics*
2. *Grades students gave themselves on work and grades I gave them*
3. *Copies of rubrics we developed*
4. *Copies of students' self-evaluations using rubrics*

Methods of Evaluation:

1. *Compare students' grades and my grades prior to using rubrics (pre-test)*
2. *Compare students' grades and my grades after using rubrics (post-test)*

Observations:

1. *Peer observations by fellow English teachers*
2. *Informal observation by principal*

Developing Research Questions

Name: _____   Date: _____

Topic: _____

Essential Question:

Related Questions:

Developing Learner-Centered Goals

Name: _____ Date: _____

Essential Question:

Professional Goals

Learner-Centered Goals

Professional Development Plan

Name: _____   Date: _____

Time frame for plan: _____

Topic selected: _____

Rationale for Selecting Topic:

Essential Question:

Related Questions:

Professional Goals:

Learner-Centered Goals:

Professional Development Plan (continued)

Baseline Data:

Action Plan (Intervention):

Documentation:

Methods of Evaluation:

Observations:

Professional Development Process

<u>Ideas</u> about the professional development process:

1. _____

2. _____

3. _____

4. _____

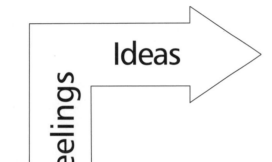

Summary Statement:

<u>Feelings</u> about the professional development process:

1. _____

2. _____

3. _____

4. _____

Chapter 3

The Resource Review

"If we conceive of teaching as an art, does theory have a role to play in the guidance and conduct of teaching? Does artistic teaching vitiate the use of scientifically grounded theory?" (Eisner 1985, 177)

The Role of Research

Eisner (1985) argues that theoretical frameworks are extremely important. Educational theory, for example, helps teachers focus on aspects of classroom life that might otherwise be neglected. Psychological theory might address questions of self-esteem, forms of reinforcement, or the need to provide students with guided practice—issues that may be neglected if the theory did not remind teachers of these issues. Glatthorn (1996, 46) agrees, saying "The professional who knows the theory and research on student motivation will be better able to develop the skills to motivate students than those who operate without that knowledge base."

Theory also gives teachers some "rough approximations of what we might expect of certain pedagogical arrangements by the kinds of generalizations that they provide" (Eisner 1985, 178). It also helps teachers plan, because theory suggests what types of circumstances could occur when these "pedagogical arrangements" are implemented.

Professional Literature

"Experience alone will not suffice as a basis for selection of problems for study. Another means of identifying educational problems is professional literature." (Turney and Robb 1971, 12)

Most teachers and administrators do not read empirical research studies in education, but they need to keep abreast of current research-based practices in education that call attention to potential problems and possible solutions to problems. Teachers do not have to conduct quantitative studies with control and experimental groups to engage in educational research. As Boileau (1993, 19) points out, ". . . Teaching is actually an expression of scholarship, scholarship that does not confine itself to the cutting edge of research, but also lives in intimate knowledge and teaching of the research in the classroom." One professional standard is that teacher candidates "know and use research-based principles of effective practice; that is, they should be able to explain why they decide to use a certain strategy and teach a particular idea a certain way" (Wise and Leibbrand 1996, 203).

Needs Assessment

"Change is meaningful when it is dictated by need recognized through practice and research. Staff development efforts should begin with a needs assessment." (Harp 1994, 309)

Since a professional development plan is just the first step in the professional development process, it is important that each individual or group takes time to review what they already *know* about their question, ask more questions about *what* they would like to find out, and then complete the professional development plan delineating *how* they plan to find the answers to their questions. The K-W-L graphic organizer created by Donna Ogle, can be adapted to create a personalized needs assessment.

Kathy's needs assessment K-W-H could contain the following:

Teachers need to keep abreast of current research-based practices that call attention to potential problems and possible solutions to problems.

Professional Development Topic: Performance Rubrics

Name: _____Kathy Brown_____   Date: _____August 1996_____

K What do you think you <u>know</u> about your target topic?	**W** <u>What</u> would you like to find out?	**H** <u>How</u> do you plan to find out?
Rubric means "red" Students can assess their own work Rubrics are hard to develop Students can develop criteria and standards It's a hot topic!	How to create authentic rubrics How to get the students involved How to make valid rubrics How to convert rubrics to traditional grades How to explain rubrics to parents	Read articles on rubrics Read books in the field Watch videos on performance assessment Attend a conference or workshop Visit teachers using rubrics

Figure 3.1

Resource Review

In addition to completing a personal needs assessment, educators, like researchers, must review the literature and the resources available. This step may be challenging because, with the exception of required graduate work or coursework for salary increases, most teachers do not engage in research. Lortie (1975, as cited in Joyce and Showers 1996) describes the "cellular" nature of schools, the isolation of practitioners that prevents faculty members from working together to find out what works and what doesn't. It is essential that practitioners pool their resources and areas of expertise and become learning communities.

Even if a person has selected a topic and goals that no one else is addressing, she will need to talk with others about what they are doing and observe people in other classrooms, schools, or communities who are implementing strategies or trying systems she might be interested in starting. People, not just books, articles, and videos, are essential resources in the inquiry process.

Gideonse (as cited in Elmore 1990, 113) states that "professional inquiry is rarely an individual enterprise. Excepting the occasional late afternoon committee meeting, however, teachers currently practice their profession in virtual isolation from one another. Schools that pursue an inquiry orientation toward teaching will have to provide opportunities for extensive professional interactions where teachers can work together to identify learning problems (and common aspirations) and devise strategies to address them."

In addition to completing a personal needs assessment, educators, like researchers, must review the literature and the resources available.

Available Resources

The teacher/researcher should begin to explore the topic and learner goals by asking the following questions:

1. Who are the experts in this area?

2. What books have been written on the subject?

3. What educational journals publish articles about this topic?

4. What videos have been produced about the topic?

5. Where would information about workshops or conferences on this topic be published?

6. Are there study groups, networks, or support groups that focus on this topic?

These questions trigger other questions that propel the investigation and sometimes lead to revisions in the original professional development plan. Educators regularly revise, update, and sometimes rewrite their plans as they learn more about the topic.

Fishbone Graphic Organizer

The fishbone graphic organizer could be used to identify sources of information that could be used to research ideas before data collection begins. Kathy might fill out her fishbone as follows:

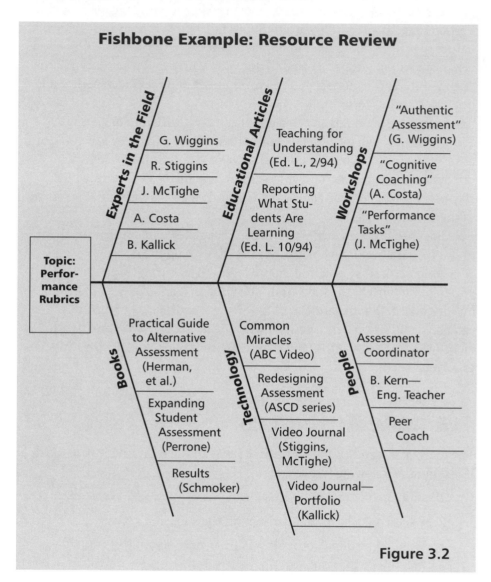

Fishbone Example: Resource Review

Experts in the Field
G. Wiggins
R. Stiggins
J. McTighe
A. Costa
B. Kallick

Educational Articles
Teaching for Understanding (Ed. L., 2/94)
Reporting What Students Are Learning (Ed. L. 10/94)

Workshops
"Authentic Assessment" (G. Wiggins)
"Cognitive Coaching" (A. Costa)
"Performance Tasks" (J. McTighe)

Topic: Performance Rubrics

Books
Practical Guide to Alternative Assessment (Herman, et al.)
Expanding Student Assessment (Perrone)
Results (Schmoker)

Technology
Common Miracles (ABC Video)
Redesigning Assessment (ASCD series)
Video Journal (Stiggins, McTighe)
Video Journal—Portfolio (Kallick)

People
Assessment Coordinator
B. Kern—Eng. Teacher
Peer Coach

Figure 3.2

After reviewing books, publications, and media, and after talking to people who have experimented with certain topics, it is important to develop a personal resource list.

Learning Lists

Another method to synthesize the important points of the resource review is to use learning lists. Learnings lists help summarize key ideas learned, things one still has to learn, activities to try, data that could be collected, and actions that will help one meet her goals (see pages 44 and 48). This list could be shared with peers during informal conferences and be included in the final portfolio.

Documentation

"Some argue, of course, that the reason practitioners do not base their practices on research is because they do not read it." (Eisner 1985, 358)

Artifacts like the article précis, book reviews, interview forms, annotated bibliographies, and workshop or conference reviews all document an educator's research about a topic. Each educator should decide which research resources are most helpful and complete the ones that will help her meet her goals.

Many of these forms of documentation can be included in the professional portfolio as evidence of preliminary research on the topic. All of these items help educators adjust their professional development plans. These artifacts also help in meeting the professional goal of discovering more about a topic in order to structure instruction to meet learner-centered goals. As Eisner (1985) states, knowing the theory helps teachers to plan and helps them to predict what types of circumstances should occur when the theory is implemented in the classroom.

Artifacts like the article précis, book reviews, interview forms, annotated bibliographies, and workshop or conference reviews all document educational research.

Examples

Article Précis

Name: _Kathy Brown_   Date: _July_

Topic: _Authentic Assessment_

Essential Question:
How can we develop valid and reliable assessments for our English students?

Bibliography (author, date, title of article, publisher, volume, number, page numbers):
Perkins, D. and T. Blythe. 1994. Putting understanding up front. Educational Leadership 51 (5): 4–7.

Summary of Key Points:
Teachers are concerned that students do not understand key concepts. Understanding is a "matter of being able to do a variety of thought-demanding things with a topic—like explaining, finding evidence and examples, generalizing, applying, analyzing, and representing the topic in a new way." These activities do not build understanding.

Reaction to Article:
I need to teach for understanding before I can assess for understanding. My assessment must be "ongoing."

Interview

Interview someone who either knows a great deal about the focus question or is experienced in implementing strategies related to the topic.

Name: _Kathy Brown_   Date: _8/15_

Person Interviewed: _Bonnie Kern_   Title: _English Teacher_

Topic: _Authentic Assessment_

1. How were you introduced to this topic?
   I took a graduate course in assessment and we had to develop new assessments for our students.

2. What are the most important things you learned?
   Involving students in the evaluation process is important. Develop rubrics with students so they know what is expected of them.

3. What advice would you give me?
   Start slowly. Do one thing at a time and maybe start with one class.

4. Can you suggest other resources I could use? *View Video Journal and ASCD tapes on assessment. Start networking.*

5. What surprised you most in your study of this area?
   How much the students loved the rubrics. Their grades went up and they rarely complained about grades.

Book Review

Name: _Kathy Brown_   Date: _8/12_

Topic: _Authentic Assessment_

Bibliography (author, date, title of article, publisher, volume, number, page numbers):
Herman, J. L., P. R. Aschbacher, and L. Winters. 1992. A practical guide to alternative assessment. Alexandria, Va.: Association for Supervision and Curriculum Development.

Key Ideas: *Alternative assessments ask students to perform, create, produce, or do something that invokes real-world applications. The terms validity, reliability, standards, criteria, dimensions were defined. The authors discussed the difference between a single or holistic score and separate ratings or analytical scoring for different aspects.*

Connections to Your Topic: *The terms discussed help connect evaluation methods used on standarized tests or the state test to what I'm doing in my English class.*

Your Reaction: *I liked learning the technical terms, because knowing the correct terminology will help me explain to students, other teachers, and parents what I'm doing.*

Learning Lists

Name: _Kathy Brown_   Topic: _Performance Rubrics_

Essential Question: _Will rubrics help students evaluate their own work?_

Key ideas I have learned . . .	Things I still need to learn . . .
criteria are the key to creating rubrics	*how to make rubrics valid and reliable*

Activities I could try . . .	Data I could collect . . .
having students develop fun rubrics to understand the process	*examples of real rubrics developed by other English classes*

Actions that will help me meet my goals . . .
1. *Find examples of writing and speech rubrics for models.*
2. *Visit a teacher who uses rubrics to see them used.*

Share these learning lists with a peer.

Peer Signature: _Lois Moss_   Date: _October_

K-W-H

Name: _____   Date: _____

Research Topic: _____

Essential Question: _____

K What do you think you <u>know</u> about your topic?	**W** <u>What</u> would you like to find out?	**H** <u>How</u> do you plan to find out?

(Strategy adapted from Donna Ogle)   © 1997 IRI/SkyLight Training and Publishing, Inc.

Fishbone

Fill in the fishbone graphic organizer by listing the possible resources you could use to research your focus goal.

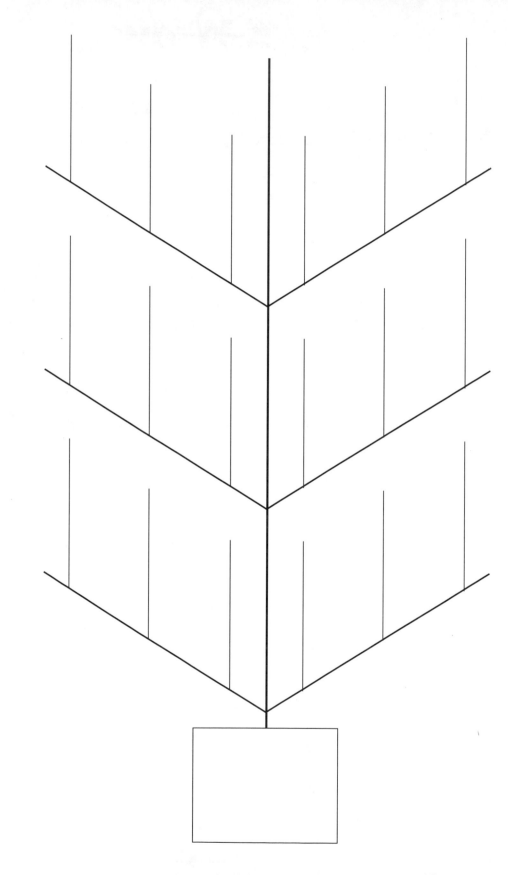

Interview

Interview someone who either knows a great deal about the focus question or is experienced in implementing strategies related to the topic.

Name: _____   Date: _____

Person Interviewed: _____   Title: _____

Topic: _____

1. How were you introduced to this topic?

2. What are the most important things you learned?

3. What advice would you give me?

4. Can you suggest other resources I could use?

5. What surprised you most in your study of this area?

Learning Lists

Name: _____ Topic: _____

Essential Question: _____

_____

Key ideas I have learned . . .	Things I still need to learn . . .

Activities I have tried . . .	Data I collected . . .

Actions that helped me meet my goals . . .

Share these learning lists with a peer.

Peer Signature: _____ Date: _____

Double-Entry Journal

How I feel about my topic <u>before</u> reviewing my resources.	How I feel about my topic <u>after</u> reviewing my resources.
Date: _____	Date: _____

Signed: _____

Chapter 4

Data Collection

"Data can help us confront what we may wish to avoid and what is difficult to perceive, trace, or gauge; data can substantiate theories, inform decisions, impel action, marshal support, thwart misperceptions and unwarranted optimism, maintain focus and goal-orientation, and capture and sustain collective energy and momentum. Data help us answer the primary question 'What do we do next?' amid the panoply of competing opportunities for action." (Schmoker 1996, 42)

Once educators have asked the essential questions, decided upon the learner-centered goals, created the professional development plan, and reviewed the available resources, they are ready to begin collecting specific artifacts. Artifacts are samples of work collected for the portfolio that document the process of trying to meet the learner goals. In the professional development portfolio, only evidence directly related to the specific goal should be collected. It is not appropriate to include awards, certificates, unrelated student artifacts, previous letters from parents and students—those items would be included in a career portfolio. Every artifact, bibliography, lesson plan, video, or letter included in this portfolio should document the process for achieving the goals listed in the professional development plan.

Where to Store?

One of the first things to decide is *where* to store the artifacts. Teachers involved in a professional portfolio pilot study in Wheeling, Illinois, said that once they established a place to store items, they began to routinely think to themselves, "This has portfolio potential." Then they would put items in their storage area until they had time to review them. Several teachers reported their regret at having thrown away so many things that they realized later could have been included in their portfolio. One teacher recommended, "Save everything. You might not include it, but sometimes the item triggers ideas you can use later when you organize the final portfolio."

Some options for storing items that might be included in the final portfolio include the following:

- **Drawer:** Set aside a drawer at home or school.

- **File Cabinet:** Use hanging files labeled "Articles," "Teacher Artifacts," "Media," "Peer Feedback," and so forth.

- **Notebook:** Use a two- or three-inch looseleaf notebook to store items.

- **Portable File Box:** These boxes can be purchased at most office supply stores. They are about six inches deep and contain racks that hold about thirty hanging files.

- **Box:** Many teachers have a designated portfolio box they keep in their classroom or at home.

- **Soft Briefcase Bag:** National conferences sometimes distribute soft bags about 11" x 14" so conference attendees can store all the handouts and educational literature.

Storage for the working portfolio does not have to be elaborate. Once the collection process is over and the selection process begins, most people organize the material formally for the final portfolio. Final portfolios can have many formats and will be discussed in more detail in later chapters.

Data are essential to school improvements because schools are, in fact, research institutions.

Data Collection

"Data help monitor and assess performance. Just as goals are an essential element of success, so data are an essential piece of working towards goals." (Schmoker 1996, 29)

The word "data" scares many educators because they equate the term with rigorous experimental studies, control groups, experimental groups, and lots of statistics! Yet data are essential to school improvements because schools are, in fact, research institutions. Brooks and Brooks (1993, 125) advise educators that to create schools that recognize, value, and respond to the cognitive, social, and emotional needs of students, they need to study those factors in their own context on an ongoing basis. "Schools have access to important data on student development all day long. We need to start systematically collecting, analyzing, and using these data to inform classroom practices."

Many educators are leery of data not only because of a discomfort with statistics but also because of the fear that if their goals have to be "measurable," they will be asked not to set goals that entail labor-intensive assessment (i.e., higher-order thinking skills, social skills) and focus instead on areas that are easily measured (i.e., spelling tests, absentee records). Many educators also fear a heavy reliance on standardized tests to measure progress at the expense of other criteria-based assesment devices like rubrics or qualitative assessments like portfolios. Fortunately, the emphasis on performance assessments gives educators many effective methods for assessing understanding, application, and thinking skills in authentic ways (Schmoker 1996).

Educators must continue to ask questions about the data they collect. Schmoker (1996, 42) suggests asking these challenging questions:

- What are the data telling us? What problems or challenges do they reveal?

- What can we do about what the data reveal? What strategies should we brainstorm? What research should we consult?

- What are the data telling us about how effective our current efforts are in helping us achieve our goals?

Baseline Data

Baseline data show "how things are" at the beginning of a study. It is difficult to measure success or failure at meeting goals at the end of the journey when no information shows where the students were at the beginning of the journey. Progress is monitored and assessed according to what changes have occurred due to specific interventions. Since this type of research is more informal than classical research, the baseline data are often informal. Examples of baseline data that can be collected at the beginning of a study are included in Figure 4.1.

The emphasis on performance assessments gives educators many effective methods for assessing understanding, application, and thinking skills in authentic ways.

Baseline Data Related to Goals

Potential Data—Beginning and End of Study

Goal: To train students in peer mediation techniques to reduce schoolwide conflicts.
- Number of discipline referrals
- Number of suspensions and expulsions
- Number of classroom and schoolwide fights
- Attitude surveys of students
- Parent questionnaires

Goal: To initiate a volunteer tutoring program to help students with mathematics.
- Questionnaires about students' attitudes towards math
- Grades in math classes of students serving as tutors
- Standardized test scores of students
- Interviews of tutors and students being tutored

Goal: To help students solve problems.
- Diagnostic test on problem solving
- Number of ways students brainstormed solutions
- Standardized tests on problem solving
- Interviews of students

Figure 4.1

Sample Baseline Data Tools

Testing
- Norm-Referenced Tests
- Criterion-Referenced Tests
- Scholastic Aptitude Tests
- Foreign Language Proficiency Tests
- Vocational Aptitude Tests

Teacher Work Samples
- Teacher-Made Tests
- Homework Assignments
- Rubrics
- Project Assignments
- Performances
- Videotaped Lessons
- Peer Observation Checklist

Questionnaires/Surveys
- Students
- Parents
- Teachers
- Administrators
- Business Leaders
- Community Leaders

Observations
- Student Work Habits
- Group Interactions
- Physical Education Skills
- Social Skills
- Problem Solving Skills
- Study Habits
- Student Motivation

Student Work Samples
- Writing
- Reading
- Math Problem Solving
- Art Work
- Group Projects
- Performance Videos

Statistics
- Student Grades
- Absentee Rates
- Referrals
- Detentions
- Drop-Out Rates
- College Admissions
- Scholarships
- Employment

Figure 4.2

Most professional development plans and portfolios used for teacher evaluation require baseline data to monitor whether goals have been met.

Figure 4.2 provides a list of baseline data tools, any of which could be used to show where students are at the beginning of the study or intervention. Often, the same instrument is used again at the end of the study to record results and determine whether educators met their goals. Teachers have always collected baseline data, perhaps without labeling it as such. Every time a teacher saves a student's writing sample or art sample from the beginning of the year, the middle of the year, and again at the end of the year, he is collecting evidence to show growth and development. If a teacher records on cassette how a student reads in September, and then records how the student reads in May, the cassette provides evidence of whether the student improved. Student portfolios have become popular largely because the portfolio profiles growth in concrete form as opposed to scattered worksheets or grade book entries. Diagnostic samples serve as evidence of a student's entry-level skills, attitudes, and feelings. Most formal professional development plans and portfolios that are used for teacher evaluation *require* baseline data in order to evaluate whether the goals have been met.

What to Collect

Educators should post learner-centered goals in their classrooms or school so they can *focus* on the items they will need to document whether they are meeting their goals. One mistake often made with student portfolios is the inclusion of only written work. Written work is one way to show understanding, but it shows only a student's verbal/linguistic abilities. Gardner's research on multiple intelligences emphasizes the need for both teachers and students to demonstrate their learnings in a variety of ways. Figure 4.3 offers an overview of the multiple intelligences with the types of learning experiences and assessments characteristic of each type of intelligence. Collecting a variety of artifacts that represents both the teacher's and the students' depth of understanding provides a more valid and reliable measurement than is provided by only one type of assessment.

How to Collect

It is important that educators consider all the possibilities of teacher-generated, student-generated, and even parent-generated artifacts that could be collected as data to monitor progress in attaining goals or serve as documentation that the goals have been met. The grid in Figure 4.4 displays a number of resources, instructional strategies, observation opportunities, assessments, reflections, and media supplements that can be collected for a professional portfolio.

Collecting a variety of artifacts that represents both the teacher's and the students' depth of understanding provides a more valid and reliable measurement than is provided by only one type of assessment.

Portfolio Collection Grid: Teacher-Generated Artifacts

Resources	Instructional Strategies	Observations
• Summaries of journal articles • Précis of books • Reviews of videotapes • Annotated bibliographies • Interviews with experts • Workshops	• Lesson plans • Unit plans • Hooks for lessons • Processing tools • Closure pieces • Mediation strategies	• Of a mentor • By a mentor • Of a peer • By a peer • By a supervisor
Media/ Technology	**Reflections**	**Assessments**
• Transparencies • Slides • Cassettes • Videotapes • Internet • E-mail • Multi-media	• Logs • Journals • Stem questions • Peer feedback • Response journals • Reflections on portfolio entries	• Quizzes • Observation checklists • Learning lists • Interviews • Teacher-made tests • Standardized tests

Figure 4.4

IRI/SkyLight Training and Publishing, Inc.

Gardner's Multiple Intelligences

Verbal/Linguistic
Speeches
Debates
Story Telling
Reports
Crosswords
Newspapers
Internet
Research
Biographies
Autobiographies
List of Books Read
Annotated Bibliographies

Visual/Spatial
Artwork
Photographs
Math Manipulatives
Graphic Organizers
Posters, Charts
Illustrations
Cartoons
Props for Plays
Use of Overhead, Blackboard
Story Boards
Videotapes
Murals
Sculptures
Models

Musical/Rhythmic
Background Music
Songs about Books, People,
    Countries, Historic Events
Raps
Jingles
Lyric Poems
Choral Reading
Tone Patterns
Trios/Quartets
Choirs
Cheers

Intrapersonal
Reflective Journals
Learning Logs
Goal-Setting Journals
Divided Journals
Metacognitive Reflections
Independent Reading
Silent Reflection Time
Self-Evaluation
Poetry Writing
Meditations
Concentration Exercises
Diaries

Logical/Mathematical
Puzzles
Outlines
Timelines
Analogies
Patterns
Problem Solving
Lab Experiments
Formulas
Abstract Symbols
Venn Diagrams
Mind Maps
Computer Games

Bodily/Kinesthetic
Field Trips
Role Playing
Learning Centers
Labs
Sports/Games
Cooperative Learning
Body Language
Experiments
Interviews
Pantomiming
Presentations
Dances
Aerobics

Interpersonal
Group Video, Film, Slides
Team Computer Programs
Think-Pair-Share
Cooperative Tasks
Jigsaws
Wrap Arounds
Electronic Mail
Class Discussions
Conversations
Interviews
Conferences

Naturalist
Outdoor Education
Environmental Studies
Field Trips (Farm, Zoo)
Field Studies
Bird Watching
Nature Walk
Weather Forecasting
Stargazing
Exploring Nature
Ecology Studies
Identifying Leaves and Rocks

(Adapted from Chapman 1993)

Figure 4.3

Learning experiences and assessments characteristic of each intelligence.

IRI/SkyLight Training and Publishing, Inc.

While Figure 4.4 displays teacher-generated artifacts, Figure 4.5 displays work samples, media supplements, assessments, and reflections that are student-generated and parent-generated. The number of resources listed also addresses the multiple intelligences of both the educators conducting the study and the students involved in the study.

"Less is more" is a philosophy that can be applied to the number of items included. Quality is better than quantity in the final portfolio and the portfolio conference.

Portfolio Collection Grid: Student-Generated Artifacts

Individual Work	Group Work	Media/Technology
• Reports • Artwork • Recordings • Graphic organizers • Stories • Problems • Experiments • Presentations • Projects	• Presentations (videotape) • Projects (pictures) • Reenactments (videotape) • Debates • Mock trials • Experiments	• Cassettes • Videotapes • Slides • Multimedia • Computer • Photographs • Internet
Reflections	**Assessments**	**Parent Reactions**
• Reflective logs • Journal entries • Portfolio reflections • Metacognitive reactions • Transfer strategies • Goal setting	• Rough drafts/Final drafts • Quizzes • Teacher-made tests • Diagnostic tests • Standardized tests • Interviews • Peer evaluations	• Notes • Letters • Phone calls • Visits • Surveys • Back-to-school nights • Conferences • PTA meetings

Figure 4.5

Artifact Selection Log

One tool to help an educator focus on why he would include a particular artifact in his portfolio is the artifact selection log. The log includes the date the item was collected, a description of the item, and the rationale for including the item in the portfolio. The rationale section asks educators to think about why this artifact either answers the research questions or provides evidence that they are on track for meeting their goals. The rationale section also helps the educator exclude items that may be interesting or attractive but which in fact do *not* give evidence to support attainment of the goal. This process helps ensure the "selection" of key artifacts rather than "collection" of everything remotely connected to the initial research question. "Less is more" is a philosophy that can be applied to the number of items included. Quality is better than quantity in the final portfolio and the portfolio conference. Educators must answer the "compelling why" as to why they are including the artifact and justify its relationship to the goal. Sample entries in artifact selection logs are given in Figure 4.6.

Artifact Selection Log Samples

Topic: Faculty Team Building

Goal: To have faculty members work in cadres to address target goals for increasing students' academic achievement.

Date	Item Collected	Rationale for Including in Portfolio
Sept. 1	Attitude survey about working in teams given to all faculty members	Use survey to anticipate problems before team-building activities. Use survey results as baseline data. Give same survey in May to see if attitudes change.

Topic: Developing Problem-Solving Skills

Goal: To help students develop problem-solving skills.

Date	Item Collected	Rationale for Including in Portfolio
Sept. 22	Diagnostic problem-solving tests from seventh-grade math students. Collect scores for each individual student, class, and whole group.	We analyzed the number as well as the sophistication of the methods used by students to solve problems. We will give the same test at the end of the study to see if students increased the variety of methods. We'll compare scores by classes because each teacher will use a different approach to teaching problem solving.

Figure 4.6

The Artifact Log documents the collection process.

IRI/SkyLight Training and Publishing, Inc.

An Ongoing Process

The collection process begins once the learner-centered goals have been established and continues until the final selection process of the final professional portfolio. People experienced in developing portfolios warn about the dangers of procrastination. Many educators regret that they did not start collecting evidence until close to the end of the year. The data showed how the students were doing in April, but no one could tell if they were improving, staying the same, or regressing because no baseline data had been collected at the beginning of the year.

The professional development plan usually contains a section for collecting diagnostic information at the beginning of the study. Once that information is recorded, it is important to date all other entries and collect follow-up data on a periodic basis to monitor the effectiveness or ineffectiveness of the intervention.

Schmoker (1996) says that even though teachers are initially wary of gathering data, they become energized when the right kind of improvement process is under way. People close to the implementation of new ideas are the big stakeholders in the process. When they see actual progress, they are even more desirous of getting better results. Gathering information is not reserved exclusively for statisticians. Most conscientious teachers or teams of teachers can collect and analyze essential data, without the help of statisticians or psychometricians. As Schmoker states, "Data can be effective tools for promoting improvement. They can never be totally accurate or reliable, but in the hands of conscientious professionals, they promote successful, goal-oriented effort" (Schmoker 1996, 43).

Most conscientious teachers or teams of teachers can collect and analyze essential data, without the help of statisticians or psychometricians.

Examples

Baseline Data

Name: *Kathy Brown* Topic: *Performance Rubrics*

Date: *Sept.* Focus: *Creating rubrics for self-assessment*

Research Questions/ Goals	Baseline Data
Students will assess their written work.	Students' assessment of their paragraphs without using rubrics (grades they gave themselves, and grades I gave them).
Students will assess their performances.	Students' assessment of their speeches (grades they gave themselves and their comments about the process).
Students will create rubrics to evaluate their work.	Copies of initial and revised rubrics.

Portfolio Collection Grid
Teacher-Generated Artifacts

Name: *Kathy Brown* Topic: *Performance Rubrics*

Resources	Instructional Strategies	Observations
Article: "Putting Understanding Up Front" (Perkins and Blythe) *Book:* Student-Centered Classroom Assessments (Stiggins) *People:* Visitation to teacher's classroom; workshop on "rubrics"	Lesson plan for introducing rubrics to students. Cooperative student groups act as "critical friends" to assess each other's work.	My observation of a teacher already using rubrics. My peer coach. The assessment coordinator observing me.

Media/Technology	Reflections	Assessments
Showed students Common Miracles tape to emphasize the importance of reflection and metacognition. Showed ASCD's Performance Assessment tape to show students how other classes developed rubrics.	Sample stems used to help students reflect on their work. Sample reflections I wrote on my work to model good reflections.	Grades and comments from the diagnostic assessment. Grades and comments from the final assessment. Questionnaires to students and parents.

Portfolio Collection Grid
Student-Generated Artifacts

Name: *Kathy Brown* Topic: *Performance Rubrics*

Individual Work	Group Work	Media/Technology
Copies of students' writing and their self-evaluations. A mini-portfolio showing improved writing from September to March.	The group's peer editing checklist used to assess their writings. Group rubrics devised to evaluate their research paper. Class rubric created to evaluate their speeches.	A videotape of the class creating the speech rubric. Videotape of 5 students giving speeches and their evaluation of their speeches.

Student Reflections	Student Assessments	Parent Reactions
Copies of students' reflections on their written work. Students' journal entries discussing self-evaluation.	Copies of diagnostic (pre-tests) and final (post-test) evaluations. Taped interviews with students.	Results of parent survey about students' self-evaluation. A taped interview with a parent of a special needs student talking about standards. A letter from a parent telling how much her daughter's enthusiasm for writing has grown.

Artifact Selection Log

Name: *Kathy Brown*

Goal: *Help students assess their work.*

Date	Item Selected	Rationale for Including in the Portfolio
Sept. 8	Results of diagnostic assessment given students the first week of school.	This is baseline data to show difficulty of students to assess their work. They didn't know the criteria— or my expectations.
Oct. 14	The first class rubric to assess their persuasive speeches. The rubric took one day to complete.	Our first effort was really difficult. We had too many criteria and didn't allow for a "0" on the scoring guide.
Feb. 10	A reflection from Bobby Mason about how he had always hated writing before he came to my class.	I probably would not have known about Bobby's conversion from hating to loving writing if I hadn't read his reflection.

Baseline Data

Name: _____   Topic: _____

Date: _____   Focus: _____

Learner-Centered Goals	Baseline Data

Portfolio Collection Grid
Teacher-Generated Artifacts

Name: _____   Topic: _____

Goal: _____

Resources	Instructional Strategies	Observations
Media/Technology	**Reflections**	**Assessments**

Portfolio Collection Grid
Student-Generated Artifacts

Name: _____   Topic: _____
Goal: _____

Individual Work	Group Work	Media/Technology

Reflections	Assessments	Parent Reactions

Artifact Selection Log

Name: _____

Goal: _____

Date	Item Selected	Rationale for Including in the Portfolio

Reflections

About a hundred years ago, American psychologist William James argued that "teaching is an art" and that research emanating from psychology or any other social science could not directly tell a teacher what to do. Berliner and Casanova (1996, ix), however, believe "Teaching *can* be studied scientifically, like any other human endeavor; and, through education and training, dramatic changes in teachers' behavior *have* resulted."

Respond to these ideas:

_____

_____

_____

_____

_____

_____

_____

_____

_____

_____

_____

_____

_____

_____

_____

_____

_____

_____

_____

_____

_____

_____

_____

Chapter 5

The Collaborative Process

"One cannot examine the literature on staff development and not notice the number of researchers, administrators, and trainers who endorse the concept of peer support or coaching. It appears that coaching is considered requisite to effective implementation of innovation." (Harp 1994, 306)

Collegiality

Trips can be more enjoyable when someone comes along to share the discovery of new ideas, to reflect on the beauty of new places, and to discuss new adventures. The professional development journey can also be more fulfilling and rewarding if invited friends come along.

As mentioned earlier, it is critical that educators collaborate throughout the entire process. Selecting goals, planning implementation, and reflecting on successes and failures are much more meaningful when they involve more than one person. Besides discussing artifacts and commenting on journals, peers, mentors, and even supervisors can observe, coach, and discuss important aspects of the professional development process.

Peer Coaching

Bernhardt (1994, 143) defines peer coaching as teachers establishing teams to work together at the classroom level. These teams establish goals that fit within the framework of the overall school goals: "They also plan for the implementation of these goals, observe in each other's classrooms, and meet in postobservation conferences to provide *positive* feedback and support for each other's implementation efforts." Bernhardt believes that the use of peer coaching requires a long-term action plan as well as effective communication skills and some means of incentive and accountability.

Learning Transfer

In addition to encouraging sharing among professionals and promoting a risk-free environment for learning new strategies, peer coaching also fosters the transfer of staff development from the textbook, inservice, or workshop to the teachers' classrooms. Bellanca (1995, 22) cites the research of Joyce and Showers that showed the positive effects of peer coaching to various models of teaching: "Their examination of the impact of peer coaching on classrooms supported the argument that when an education program for teachers does not provide a peer coaching follow-up, the program is a waste of dollars and time. If nothing else, programs without peer coaching produce minimal personal and organizational change" (see Figure 5.1).

Despite research on the positive effects of peer coaching and its tremendous potential in professional development, it has not been widely used or accepted as a viable professional development tool.

Effects of Staff Development

Training Strategy	Classroom Application		
	Knowledge	Demonstration of Behavior	Transfer to Work Setting
Presentation of Concepts and Theory	85%	15%	10%
Demonstration of Behavior	85%	18%	10%
Low-Risk Practice with Feedback (Micro- Teaching)	85%	80%	15%
Coaching in Work Setting (Re: Behavior and Decisions)	90%	90%	80%

(Adapted from Joyce and Showers 1988, as cited in Bellanca 1995, 23)

Figure 5.1

Despite research on the positive effects of peer coaching and its tremendous potential in professional development, it has not been widely used or accepted as a viable professional development tool. As McGreal says, "No matter how much we've heard about peer coaching, I haven't seen any increase in the amount of peer coaching going on. It just isn't happening, particularly in middle, junior, and senior high schools. Part of it is just time and energy, and the logistics of getting teachers released to visit each other, to work together. So I'm finding that it works for the administrator to be responsible for getting the group together, for assisting the team in building their plan, for being available to coach and encourage" (as cited in Brandt 1996, 33).

If peer coaching is going to give teachers feedback on how they are meeting their professional goals, administrators have to structure the program carefully. They need to train teachers in observation skills, mediation skills, conferencing skills, and collaborative skills. They also need to schedule time for teachers to plan the observation and to hold post-conference discussions.

Cognitive Coaching

In their book *Cognitive Coaching: A Foundation for Renaissance Schools*, Costa and Garmston (1994, as cited in Harp 1994) use the term *cognitive coaching* to define "a nonjudgmental process—built around a planning conference, observation, and a reflecting conference. Anyone in the educational setting can become a cognitive coach—teachers, administrators, department chairs, or support personnel. A coaching relationship may be established between teacher and teacher, administrator and teacher, and/or administrator and fellow administrator. When a cognitive coaching relationship is established between two professionals with similar roles, or peers, it can be referred to as *peer coaching*" (2).

Harp describes coaching as a break from the traditional adversary model where supervisors are charged with bringing about change through the supervision of the workers. Instead, the coaching model emphasizes collaboration, the sense that "we are all learners," and the resources of all people within the school. The ultimate goal of coaching is for both the teacher and the coach to learn so that the students will ultimately benefit.

As defined by Costa and Garmston, the coaching process consists of the four phases displayed in Figure 5.2.

The ultimate goal of coaching is for both the teacher and the coach to learn so that the students will ultimately benefit.

The Coaching Process

Phase 1 Planning Conference
The teacher to be observed (1) clarifies lesson, goals, and objectives, (2) shares anticipated teaching strategies, (3) identifies data to be collected on student achievement, and (4) identifies data the coach is to collect during the lesson.

Phase 2 The Lesson
Coach gathers the data identified in Phase 1.

Phase 3 Reflecting
The teacher shares impressions of and critiques the lesson, identifying data used for conclusions.

Phase 4 Application Phase
The coach has the teacher identify what was learned, draw implications for future lessons, and give impression of the coaching process.

(Adapted from Harp 1994, 309. Reprinted with permission.)

Figure 5.2

Coaching differs from traditional evaluation of teachers in many ways. First, evaluation is usually conducted by supervisors for the purposes of "quality control," whereas coaching can be done by a wide assortment of people throughout the year for the purpose of improving instruction. In coaching, the data collected goes to the teacher—not the district office—for the purpose of self-evaluation. Costa and Garmston (1994, as cited in Harp) have developed a chart (see Figure 5.3, page 68) that makes additional distinctions between coaching and evaluation.

Coaching/Evaluation Distinctions

Attribute	Coaching	Evaluation
Who's responsible?	It is possible to delegate this responsibility to department chairpersons, peers, mentors, or colleagues.	By law, only personnel holding an administrative credential may be authorized to evaluate.
Timing	Coaching starts with the first day on the job and can be ongoing throughout the year.	Districts adopt policies and deadlines by which teacher must be evaluated.
Purposes	Improve instruction, curriculum, and student learning.	Quality control and meeting contractual requirements.
Sources of Criteria	The teacher determines what the coach shall look for as criteria for excellence in terms of student behavior and teacher behavior.	Quality teaching standards are usually developed, negotiated, adopted, and made public on forms which are used in the evaluation process. While these statements vary from district to district, it is common for an evaluator to rate teachers' performance on these criteria.
Uses of the Data Collected	The data collected is given to the teacher.	Information written on the district-adopted forms are usually distributed to the teacher, to the district for placement in the employee's personnel file, and another copy is retained by the building principal.
Topics Covered	Learning, classroom interaction, instruction, student performance, curriculum adherence, individual student behavior, teachers' behavior and skills, etc.	In addition, may include such performance as punctuality, willingness to participate in extracurricular and professional activities, personal characteristics, professional attitudes, and growth, etc.
Value Judgments	The teacher evaluates her own performance according to the criteria that were set out in the planning conference.	Within the word "evaluation" is "value." Teacher performance is rated by evaluations such as Outstanding, Adequate, or Needs to Improve.
The Role of the Observer	The teacher informs the coach of what to look for and what feedback information would be desired and helpful.	Equipped with the criteria from the district's evaluation system, the observer knows what to look for before entering the classroom. Evaluators are often trained in techniques of observing classroom instruction so that they can detect indicators of excellence or inadequacies in the specified performance criteria.
Empowerment	The power to coach is bestowed by the teacher. They "allow" themselves to be coached because of the respect, the helpfulness, and the leadership qualities of the coach.	The power to evaluate is bestowed by the Board of Trustees and the State or Province. It is a line staff authority position.

(From Costa and Garmston 1994, as cited in Harp 1994, 308. Reprinted with permission.)

Figure 5.3

Peer/Cognitive Coaching Plan

Prior to observations, the person being observed and the peer or cognitive coach should meet to plan (page 71 shows an example). They should discuss the target goal of the observations as well as the types of data to be collected. Is the observer going to tally specific behaviors of students? Is the observer going to write down the types of questions the teacher asks or perhaps note the students' reactions to the teacher's strategies? They should also set a time for the post-conference to discuss the lesson.

The Power of the Peer

The value of working in teams and the importance of collegiality cannot be underestimated. Research studies support the importance of educators communicating and supporting each other in order to achieve common goals. Lortie (1975, as cited in Schmoker 1996) saw the negative effects of teacher isolation in the "hermetically sealed world of classrooms." He found that "individualism combines with presentism to retard the search for occupational knowledge. Teachers who work in isolation cannot create an empirically grounded, semantically potent common language. Unless they develop teams to indicate specific events, discussions will lack the clarity needed to enlighten practice . . ." (10). Fullan (1991, 132) found that "collegiality among teachers, as measured by the frequency of communication, mutual support, help, etc., was a strong indicator of implementation success. Virtually every research study on the topic has found this to be the case."

Peers can provide valuable written and oral feedback to items that may or may not be included in the final portfolio.

Professional Development Plan

An ongoing feedback loop is essential for the success of a professional development plan and a professional portfolio. The feedback could be in the form of more formal peer and cognitive coaching, or it could be more informal, like the conversations between colleagues or the sharing of artifacts.

The example on page 71 shows how professionals can elicit feedback from other professionals during informal observations. In a pre-observation conference the person to be observed discusses her goal with the colleague and asks the colleague to observe specific areas. Later, after the observation, they meet informally to discuss the observation.

Artifact Discussions

In addition to peer coaching and cognitive coaching, professionals can also elicit valuable feedback in an informal setting by discussing artifacts or samples of things they have developed to meet professional goals. The ultimate artifact is the entire portfolio, but peers can provide valuable written and oral feedback to items that may or may not be included in the final portfolio.

Examples of artifacts that could be used to elicit conversations about professional goals include the following:

- Instructional units
- Teacher-made tests
- Letters to parents
- Pictures of classroom and students
- Cassette tape of tutoring session

- Video of student performances
- List of class rules and consequences
- Programs from school assemblies
- Student test scores
- Strategic plans

Artifacts provide fertile ground for conversations related to the product, the process, and the potential for meeting individual goals. It is important to save everything that has "discussion potential." The collection process is indiscriminate. The next step—the selection process—will allow individuals to re-examine the items collected and choose significant items for the final portfolio. The example on page 71 shows other examples of artifact discussions.

Artifacts provide fertile ground for conversations related to the product, the process, and the potential for meeting individual goals.

The Coaching Process

Name: _Kathy Brown_   Topic: _Helping Students Create a Rubric_

Peer Coach: _Lois_

Phase One: Planning Conference (The teacher identifies the following:)

1. Lesson Goals: *Students will learn to create a rubric to assess their writing*
2. Anticipated Teaching Strategies: *Model how to generate criteria*
3. Data to be Collected on Student Achievement: *Their final products*
4. Data collected by the Coach: *Students' level of understanding*

Phase Two: The Lesson (The coach gathers data.)

Time _8:45_ Number of students who seem confused (_3_)

Time _9:15_ Number of students who seem confused (_8_)

Phase Three: Reflecting (Teacher shares impressions and critiques the lesson using data.)

I should have grouped students to brainstorm criteria and to complete their first rubric for writing. I skipped from a whole-class example to their individual work. I needed a group example in the middle.

Phase Four: Application Phase (The teacher identifies learnings and implications for future lessons.)

Check that students know what criteria to use to describe writing before they do a rubric.

Peer Coaching Possibilities

Invite someone to observe and tell you how well you meet your goals.

Focus Goal	Observations
Developing effective facilitation skills	*You are meeting with parents who are upset with changes to the school report card. Have someone observe specific facilitation skills you use.*
Developing proactive strategies to prevent potential discipline problems	*You are trying management strategies you have studied. Ask a colleague to observe a class and record when you:* *1. Use proximity.* *2. Redirect students' attention* *3. Prevent possible disruptions*

Artifact Discussions

Name: _Mark Green_   Date: _Nov. 6_

Focus Goal: _Problem-Solving_   Colleague: _Pete Faust_

Document the discussion with your colleague by filling in the following:

Focus Goal	Artifact	Discussion Questions from Colleague
Implement portfolios	*A sample student portfolio in math class*	*1. How did you organize your portfolio system?* *2. How did the students/parents like the portfolios?* *3. Could you see the students' growth over time?* *4. What woul you change next time?*
Design a six-week problem-based learning unit for science class	*A proposal to the city council to remove hazardous waste from the city*	*1. How did students select the problem?* *2. What resources were needed for the project?* *3. What special problems were encountered?* *4. How will you grade the group project?* *5. Would you do this again?*

Peer Coaching Plan

Observee: _Pat Smith_   Observer: _Mark_

Pre-Conference Date: _11/6_ Observation Date: _11/8_

Target Goal of Observation:
Tally the types of questions I ask students.

Number of recall questions: ____ |||| |||| ||||

Number of processing questions: ____ |||| ||||

Number of application questions: ____ |||

Post-Conference Date: _11/9_ ____

Observer's Feedback:
You asked 15 recall questions. You also did not give students enough wait time to answer processing and application questions.

Response from Observee:
I need to ask higher-level questions and allow more time for students to think about their answers—especially if the questions require more thought.

The Coaching Process

Name: _____   Topic: _____

Peer Coach: _____

Phase One: Planning Conference (The teacher identifies the following:)

1. Lesson Goals:

2. Anticipated Teaching Strategies:

3. Data to be Collected on Student Achievement:

4. Data Collected by the Coach:

Phase Two: The Lesson (The coach gathers data.)

Phase Three: Reflecting (Teacher shares impressions and critiques the lesson using data.)

Phase Four: Application Phase (The teacher identifies learnings and implications for future lessons.)

Peer Coaching Possibilities

Invite a peer to observe your teaching and provide feedback on how well you are meeting your goals.

Focus Goal	Peer Observations

Artifact Discussions

Name: _____ Date: _____

Focus Goal: _____ Colleague: _____

Document the discussion with your colleague by filling in the following:

Focus Goal	Artifact	Discussion Questions from Colleague

Peer Coaching Plan

Observee: _____   Observer: _____

Pre-Conference Date: _____   Observation Date: _____

Target Goal of Observation:

Observer's Feedback:

Response from Observee:

Artifact Journal

Name: _____   Date: _____

Peer: _____   Date: _____

Description of Artifact	Peer Reaction to Artifact
Your Reaction to Artifact	

Chapter 6

Selection and Organization

"Teachers should keep a portfolio because it assists in overall growth, not because it is a duty. Teaching is a very demanding professional role; the portfolio should assist in the performance of that role, not become one more burden." (Glatthorn 1996, 35)

Selection Process

The selection process is the fourth major step in the portfolio process and revolves around these key questions:

- Who will be selecting?
- What will be selected?
- When will the items be selected?
- Why are the items selected?

Who Will Select?

Even though the portfolio allows an educator to have a stake in his own professional development, it doesn't necessarily mean that he is the only one who can select items for the final portfolio. The collaborative nature of the entire portfolio process encourages "other voices" to be heard. Every educator should consider the following players in the selection process:

- Portfolio Creators—They can select the significant items that show they are meeting their goals.

- Mentors—They can use their expertise to select items that they think represent the progress made by the portfolio creator.

- Peers—They can provide insight as objective observers about the changes they see in the portfolio creator and the students.

- Supervisors—They might select items that reflect school goals and can be used for accountability assessment and performance review.

- District Personnel—They may want to require some standard pieces from all personnel to gauge the impact of the research on all the students in the district.

- Students—They may want to select items that reflect their accomplishments.

- Parents/Community Members—They may want to include items that meet a school goal that they are concerned with (i.e., test scores, reading improvement).

Regardless of who is involved in the final selection process, it is important that the creator of the portfolio "reach out" and solicit feedback from others. The tradition of teacher isolation needs to evolve into teacher communities where no one is an island—everyone is a member of the whole community of learners and receptive to the ideas, insights, and reflections of others.

What Will Be Selected?

One of the most common problems with portfolios, both for students and for educators, is the collection of *too much* stuff! Portfolios often become large and cumbersome notebooks filled with scores of items because people do not take the time to select the significant items that represent key learnings, the greatest challenge, the most growth, or the biggest surprise.

So often, educators overwhelm job interviewers or supervisors with a 25-pound portfolio. It is like going to a neighbor's house for dinner only to be subjected to a video barrage, a 150-slide slideshow, or a double-wide photo album of a vacation in Europe. Ten pictures of the Eiffel Tower can border on overkill. One picture of the Tower with the tourist's reactions upon seeing the Tower for the first time is more meaningful than ten pictures without any commentary. In selecting items for inclusion, educators will do well to heed the advice Gertrude Stein supposedly offered the young Ernest Hemingway—"Less is more."

Selective Abandonment

Costa warns educators about overloading the curriculum and crowding out the essential learning pieces. His advice could also apply to developers of professional portfolios. One young student teacher was told to review all the artifacts she had collected and focus on just a few important ones to take for a job interview. She told her supervising teacher, "It's all so good—I can't possibly eliminate anything." She was disappointed, however, when the principal who interviewed her said he didn't have time to preview her fifty-page portfolio because he was on a tight schedule. She realized that the "less is more" philosophy was right and that if she had selected two or three critical items, perhaps the principal would have been more inclined to discuss them with her.

Regardless of who is involved in the final selection process, it is important that the creator of the portfolio "reach out" and solicit feedback from others.

Critical Pieces

The final selection process involves reviewing everything that has been collected throughout the year and selecting fifteen to twenty key items. For example, an administrator focusing on team-building among his faculty might have collected many artifacts throughout a year, but he would review the collection and select critical pieces that best represent his attempts to achieve the focus goal. The portfolio creator would then write about the significance of each item selected or give the rationale of why it was selected instead of other "collectibles."

Items Collected
for a Principal's Portfolio on Team Building

- Five memos to staff highlighting research on team building.

- Pictures of three team building activities in faculty meetings.

- Minutes of faculty team-building meetings.

- Videotape of skit to symbolize each team's work.

- Audio cassette interview of ten faculty discussing the effectiveness of team-building efforts.

- Results of a faculty survey of the effectiveness of bonding efforts.

- The principal's reflections on the effectiveness of his strategies and ideas for follow-up activities.

Figure 6.1

After reviewing the various pieces collected (Figure 6.1), the principal would carefully select five to seven items that best reflect his efforts to achieve his focus goal of building effective teacher teams. Figure 6.2 (page 80) shows the artifacts selected and the rationale for selecting them.

When to Select?

There is no set time table for the selection process. Some people prefer to select final items throughout the year. Each time they meet with peers, they discuss the collections and select items for inclusion. Others prefer to wait until the end of the year to review everything that has been collected and select the key items from the entire collection. The only warning is not to wait until the very last minute, because the selection process is only the first step towards metacognition: the second step entails reflecting on *why* the item was selected and writing about the impact the item has had on the students, the staff, or school programs. It takes time to think! Writing *all* the reflections in one all-nighter the night before the final portfolio confer-

The final selection process involves reviewing everything that has been collected throughout the year and selecting fifteen to twenty key items.

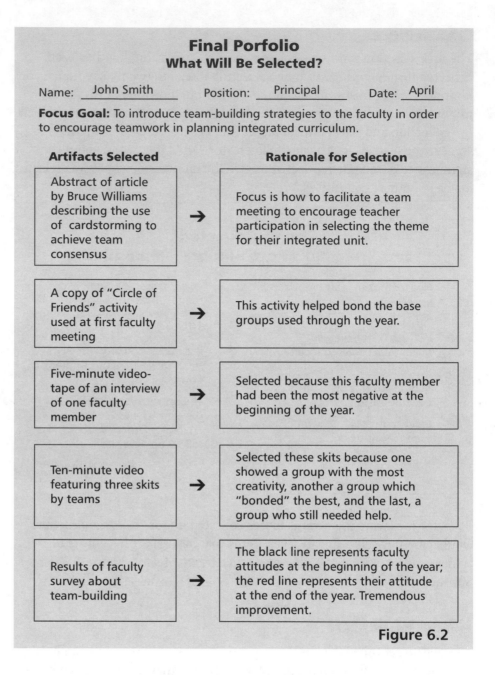

Final Porfolio
What Will Be Selected?

Name: ___John Smith___   Position: ___Principal___   Date: ___April___

Focus Goal: To introduce team-building strategies to the faculty in order to encourage teamwork in planning integrated curriculum.

Artifacts Selected		Rationale for Selection
Abstract of article by Bruce Williams describing the use of cardstorming to achieve team consensus	→	Focus is how to facilitate a team meeting to encourage teacher participation in selecting the theme for their integrated unit.
A copy of "Circle of Friends" activity used at first faculty meeting	→	This activity helped bond the base groups used through the year.
Five-minute video-tape of an interview of one faculty member	→	Selected because this faculty member had been the most negative at the beginning of the year.
Ten-minute video featuring three skits by teams	→	Selected these skits because one showed a group with the most creativity, another a group which "bonded" the best, and the last, a group who still needed help.
Results of faculty survey about team-building	→	The black line represents faculty attitudes at the beginning of the year; the red line represents their attitude at the end of the year. Tremendous improvement.

Figure 6.2

Educators need to consider the purpose of the portfolio, revisit their goals, and review the reasons as to why a particular artifact would be selected for the final portfolio.

ence is not conducive to reflective practice. The timelines for selection could be established by a school-wide policy or left up to each individual or team.

Why Select?

Various criteria exist for the selection process. Educators need to consider the purpose of the portfolio, revisit their goals, and review the reasons given in Figure 6.3 as to *why* a particular artifact would be selected for the final portfolio.

Criteria for Selection Process

An artifact is selected because it . . .

- is required by school, district, or state

- meets an objective, goal, outcome, competency, or standard

- demonstrates an increase in students' achievement

- exemplifies students' growth

- shows the "process" and the "product"

- demonstrates students' understanding of key concepts

- illustrates increased student motivation

- depicts a "watershed" event

- changed someone's teaching philosophy

- showed surprising results

Figure 6.3

The Organization Process

Once the items for the final portfolio have been selected, it is time to organize the "Showcase Portfolio" for the final conference and/or exhibition. The configuration of the final portfolio is usually left up to the individual, but the following guidelines might prove helpful.

The Showcase Portfolio

Each individual can select the "container" for the final portfolio. Some of the options include:

- Zipper Bag
- Looseleaf Notebook
- Report Folder
- Video Portfolio
- Computer Disks
- Portable File Case
- Decorated Box
- Pocket Folder

Cover

The portfolio cover expresses something about the person who created the portfolio or about the focus goal. One can use artwork, graphics, computer images, pictures, symbols, etc., to design a cover. Some people create personal images that relate to their lives or positions; others choose symbolic images; still others relate the cover to their students. The cover sets the tone for the entire portfolio and provides visual appeal.

Motif

A *motif* in literature or music is a theme or image that runs throughout a book or a composition to unify the disparate elements. On the cover of a professional portfolio, a motif works in just the same way. For example, one New York middle school teacher drew a yellow brick road on her cover.

Inside, the teacher explained her cover for the benefit of those who would look at the cover without hearing her explanation of its significance. Throughout the portfolio, sections of the yellow brick road appeared, symbolizing the steps on her journey to incorporate authentic assessment in her classes. Another teacher used puzzle pieces as a motif on his portfolio cover, showing a picture of his class cut into puzzle pieces. Throughout the portfolio, separate puzzle pieces were introduced as he tried a new item with his students. At the end, the pieces all joined together to show the whole picture of his class.

Table of Contents

The table of contents shows the writer and the reader what is contained in the final portfolio. The table of contents is useful during conferences because people can select the items they want to discuss without paging through the entire portfolio looking for key items.

Graphics

Artwork, computer graphics, symbols, cut-out art, and paste-on art can add visual appeal to a portfolio. It also can invite the reader to enter the portfolio and meet the author. Since visual/spatial is one of Gardner's multiple intelligences, everyone is encouraged to create a portfolio that is visually appealing as well as educationally informative.

Goals

Educators often include a goals page in their portfolios to record their new goals for the next year or for the next portfolio. Sometimes they set short-term or long-term goals so they have benchmarks along the way. Goals provide a clear target for the future as well as a review of accomplishments of the past. Figure 6.4 shows an example of a goal-setting web.

Self-Evaluation

Depending on whether the portfolio is used for a final performance review or for professional growth, educators often complete formal or informal evaluations using checklists, scoring rubrics, or narrative questions to analyze how they think they did in the portfolio process. They could measure whether they achieved their learner-centered, personal, or professional goals, or identify their greatest achievement. Sometimes the self-evaluation is just a checklist to monitor their progress in achieving their long-term goals. Educators need to stop, reflect, self-assess, and redirect as needed in their pursuit of focus goals and professional growth.

Educators need to stop, reflect, self-assess, and redirect as needed in their pursuit of focus goals and professional growth.

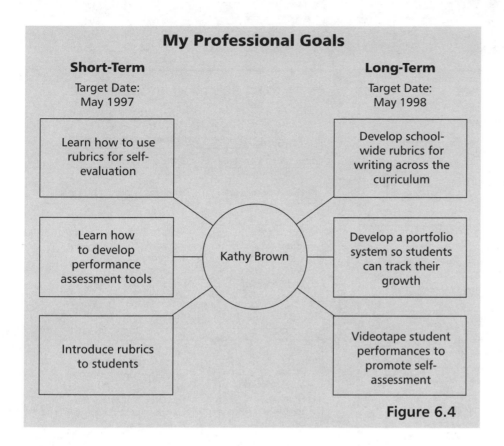

My Professional Goals

Short-Term
Target Date:
May 1997

Long-Term
Target Date:
May 1998

Learn how to use rubrics for self-evaluation

Develop school-wide rubrics for writing across the curriculum

Learn how to develop performance assessment tools

Kathy Brown

Develop a portfolio system so students can track their growth

Introduce rubrics to students

Videotape student performances to promote self-assessment

Figure 6.4

The selection process requires educators to use their metacognitive strategies, "to think about their thinking," to think about what they have learned from the particular items they plan to include.

Bibliography

A bibliography provides documentation of the resources used in investigating one's focus topic. The bibliography could include books, articles, videos, people interviewed, television programs, newscasts, radio programs, or any other sources that were helpful to the portfolio owner. It also provides sources to other people who are interested in pursuing similar goals and would like some idea of how to get started.

Selection = Metacognition

The selection process requires educators to use their metacognitive strategies, "to think about their thinking," to think about what they have learned from the particular items they plan to include. People who want to include *everything* are not taking the time or using reflective practice to cull through all the items collected to select the things that made a difference. As Danielson (1996, 39) states, "Assembling items for a portfolio is a powerful vehicle for professional reflection and analysis. When a teacher decides to include one instructional unit over another or the video of a certain class instead of another, that judgment requires determining how the features of one unit are superior to others. 'What makes it good?' 'How could it be strengthened even further?' These thought processes, particularly if accompanied by discussion, enable a teacher to enhance instructional decisions."

Examples

Portfolio Planner

Name: _Kathy Brown_

Who will select items? →
1. Kathy Brown
2. Peer—Lois
3. Students
4. Department chairperson

What items will be selected? →
1. Student-created rubric
2. Fun rubrics
3. Students' evaluations of their papers
4. Students' speech self-evaluation

When will these items be selected? →
1. October—faculty meeting
2. December—peer meeting
3. February—faculty meeting
4. March—last peer meeting

Why were these items selected? →
1. Four items met goals
2. One is my favorite
3. One changed my philosophy
4. Two were challenging

Artifact Selection and Rationale

Name: _Kathy Brown_   Position: _English Teacher_

Learner Goals: _Students will develop criteria and rubrics in order to evaluate their own work._

Artifact Selected	Rationale for Selection
Rubric for assessing a letter to the editor in the Red Badge of Courage unit.	The students created the rubric. They felt they did a better job on the assignment.
Picture of a mock trial of General Lee performed by one group.	I was surprised how professional the performance was. The students followed the rubric they created and kept rehearsing to get all 4's.

Final Portfolio: Organization

- Creative Cover
- Table of Contents
- 15–20 Artifacts
- Reflections on Each Item
- Goal-Setting Web
- Self-Evaluation of Portfolio (Rubric)
- Bibliography

The Creative Process

Your Creative Cover Ideas
- Collages
- Drawings
- Computer Graphics
- Photographs

Ideas for a Motif or Theme
- Puzzle Pieces
- Symbols
- Quotes

Graphics Options
- Clip Art
- Abstract Design
- Layouts

My Professional Goals

Short-Term Goals

Target Date: _____

Long-Term Goals

Target Date: _____

_____
Name

Portfolio Planner

Name: _____

Who will select
items? →

What items will
be selected? →

When will these
items be selected? →

Why were these
items selected? →

Artifact Selection and Rationale

Name: _____   Position: _____

Learner Goals: _____

_____

Artifact Selected	**Rationale for Selection**

The Creative Process

Cover Ideas

Motif

Graphics

Showcase Portfolio

You can bring only *four* items from your portfolio to an interview for a new position. Write your rationale for selecting each item.

Item:	Item:
Rationale:	Rationale:
Item:	Item:
Rationale:	Rationale:

Chapter 7

The Reflective Practitioner

"The process of looking at one's development through a portfolio process functions like a literal mirror—when one sees one's own image or performance—the literal reflection sparks internal reflection." (Diez 1994, 10)

The Reflection Process

"Reflection is a process of thinking systematically and insightfully about professional issues." (Glatthorn 1996, 27)

The reflection process is critical to developing the professional portfolio. Educators need to become reflective practitioners if they are to grow as professionals. Without written commentaries, explanations, and reflections, the portfolio is no more than a notebook of artifacts or a scrapbook of teaching mementos. Such a portfolio does not reveal the criteria for collecting the contents, the thoughts of why the items were selected, or what the teacher and the students learned. Even though many of these thoughts might surface in a conference, it cannot be assumed that the person who created the portfolio will always be present to discuss them. Sometimes the portfolio needs to be self-explanatory.

Wolf (1996, 36) believes that reflective commentaries are important parts of portfolios and do more than describe the portfolio contents: "They examine the teaching documented in the portfolio and reflect on what teacher and students learned." Glatthorn (1996) believes that the process of reflection begins with awareness—an awareness of teachers' feelings and thoughts; an awareness of their teaching decisions; and an awareness of their students' reactions.

Metacognition

"An intellect is someone whose mind matches itself."—Albert Camus

Metacognition—thinking about thinking—is an essential component of professional growth. Fogarty (1994) uses the example of a person reading and getting to the bottom of the page, when a little voice inside his head says, "I don't know what I just read!" With the awareness of knowing that he doesn't know, he employs a recovery strategy of reading the last sentences of each paragraph, scanning the page, looking for key words, or rereading the entire page. After using one or more strategies, he captures the meaning and continues.

Teachers are generally aware of their thinking every time they teach a lesson. They start at the planning stage, where they stand outside the situation and imagine the actual lesson and the students' reactions. Once they begin the actual lesson, they monitor and adjust as needed. Sometimes they sense total confusion on the faces of students, so they stop and clarify or reteach. Teachers monitor students' reactions and adjust instruction on an ongoing basis. "Whenever we watch student behaviors and log the information for 'minor adjustments or repairs'—we act metacognitively— beyond the cognitive" (Fogarty 1994, ix). It is as if we "freeze frame" the teaching to take a second look at what is going on. This awareness level is metacognition.

Metacognition also entails evaluating what one knows, how one knows it, and why one knows it. Fogarty uses the example of remembering something memorized years ago—a poem, lines from Shakespeare, or a nursery rhyme. She asks people to think about how they learned the piece and why they are able to recite it accurately and instantly today. Did they write it many times? Did they visualize the words on the page? Did they recite it aloud over and over again? Metacognitive reflection is "thinking how you learn and being able to generalize those skills and strategies for transfer and use into diverse situations" (Fogarty 1994, x). Costa (1991, 87) describes metacognition as "our ability to know what we know and what we don't know." Costa also describes metacognition as occurring when a person having an "inner dialogue" stops to evaluate her decision-making and problem-solving process.

Metacognition entails evaluating what one knows, how one knows it, and why one knows it.

Metacognitive Reflections

The "inner dialogue" that Costa describes occurs in schools all the time. Principals experience it when they introduce a new report card format— "How will parents react? Will the teachers feel it's too time consuming?" Teachers experience the "inner dialogue" every time they teach a lesson or try a different classroom management technique—"How will Jimmy react to these consequences? How will my third period students manage their portfolios?" This "inner dialogue" is transferred to the portfolio in the form of a written commentary or reflective entry that captures on paper the thoughts running through an educator's head. The very act of writing the thoughts helps to clarify them. Additionally, sharing thoughts with peers provides a different perspective as well as constructive feedback.

Metacognitive reflections are key elements of professional portfolios and professional growth. Without such reflections, a portfolio is only a "notebook of stuff."

Other Metacognitive Tools

Metacognitive reflections come in many shapes and sizes. Written commentaries are not the only methods of exploring the "inner thoughts" of an educator. The following tools may add variety to the reflection process.

Reflective Stems

One method that encourages reflection is the reflective stem. The stem is a statement that triggers ideas and asks the practitioner to finish the thought about a particular piece in the portfolio.

Possible Stems

1. This piece represents a watershed moment for me because . . .
2. This piece did not work for me because . . .
3. This artifact taught me something insightful about myself (or a student) because . . .
4. This piece was a stretch for me because . . .

The questions stimulate thought. The stems also encourage practitioners to include ideas that did not work and tell why. Sometimes the "disasters" cause people to rethink ideas and reflect on current practices more than a series of successful pieces will.

Artifact Registry

Dietz (1993, Facilitator's Guide, IV-7) suggests using an artifacts and evidences registry to list any artifacts and evidences that cause people to reflect on their question. The page would contain the following:

Registry Item:

Date:

Description:

Why It Belongs in the Portfolio:

Removed from Portfolio Date:

Reason for Removal and Outcomes:

This registry provides ongoing documentation of what items are included in the portfolio, the rationale for how items meet the person's goals, and an explanation of why items no longer meet the goals and have been removed.

Metacognitive reflections are key elements of professional portfolios. Without such reflections, a portfolio is only a "notebook of stuff."

The decision to include or exclude items in a portfolio is in itself a reflective process. What were the criteria for selection? Why did an item meet the criteria at one time, but then lose its status? What changed in the learner or the process?

The "X" Files—What's Hot, What's Not

Another idea for monitoring the collection/selection process would be to keep track of only those items that are excluded from the working portfolio. The items that are left in will be explained and reflected upon in the final portfolio, but it would be interesting to know what didn't make the final cut and why it wasn't deemed worthy of inclusion in the final portfolio. The rationale of why the item was excluded provides metacognitive insight into the "inner thinkings" of the portfolio owner (see Figure 7.1).

Portfolio Rejection Log

Name: Kathy Brown   Focus Topic: Authentic Assessment

Date	Rejected Item	Rejection Rationale
Sept. 16	Rubric to assess the visual aids used in speeches.	It was an early attempt. We used vague descriptors like "good visuals," "adequate design," "creative ideas" without knowing what the words meant. We couldn't grade the visual aids reliably.
Oct. 3	Abstract of "Why Authentic Assessment?" by Sid Smith.	I thought this was good because it defined assessment. After further reading, however, I found that it just talks about theory—others describe actual tools to use.

Figure 7.1

The biography of a work delineates the steps a person or group went through to arrive at a final product or performance.

Biography of a Work

Another method for reflecting on one's selections is to review the steps in the process. When the final selections appear in the portfolio, someone looking at the selections has very little information about the steps the person took to arrive at the final products—unless that person is there to explain the process. Sometimes, even the portfolio owner cannot remember the steps because the selections were made at an earlier time or she did not monitor her actions metacognitively! The biography of a work delineates the steps a person or group went through to arrive at a final product or performance. This tool can also be used to chronicle the steps in the entire portfolio process (see Figure 7.2, page 94).

Often, the initial reaction may be amended after the teacher gauges students' reactions or assesses the effectiveness of a lesson.

Biography of a Work Log

Name: ___Kathy Brown___   Focus Topic: ___Authentic Assessment___

Task: ___Creating a Teacher-Made Test___

Date	Creating a Teacher-Made Test
Feb. 2	Asked students for 5 questions on 3" x 5" cards about *Red Badge of Courage*.
Feb. 3	Used student questions to develop ten matching items, ten fill-in-the-blanks, five true-false, and three essay questions.
Feb. 4	Added a Civil War mind-map question where students mapped major battles.
Feb. 5	Added point values; timed the test; added a bonus question; added instructions and choices for different learning styles.
Feb. 6	Gave the test. The students were excited to see some of their questions on the test.

Figure 7.2

Sticky Note Reflections

One of the easiest ways to reflect on a lesson or artifact quickly and succinctly is to use different sizes of sticky notes to attach thoughts. Some people use the 3" x 5" size; others prefer the 4" x 6" style with lines. The advantage of using the notes is that a person can record an immediate reaction to an artifact, lesson, or article and then go back later and expand or amend the ideas before writing the final reflection. Often, the initial reaction may be amended after the teacher gauges students' reactions or assesses the effectiveness of a lesson. Sometimes it is effective to attach two reflections to an artifact. The first dated entry describes how the educator felt the day a lesson or strategy was introduced; the second entry, dated days or weeks later, describes how the educator felt after reflecting on the results or after hearing student reactions.

Example

Feb. 7   Reflection
Gave the *Red Badge of Courage* test today. Students were excited to see some of the questions they had submitted.

Feb. 14   Reflection
Their scores on the *Red Badge* test were the best this year. The students said the test was fair and comprehensive. It's worth taking the time to write an authentic test.

Mirror Reflections

Often times a sticky note does not allow enough space for metacognitive reflection on an artifact. It may provide the initial thoughts, but upon further reflection, the author decides to elaborate on the entry. One of the most effective ways to "dig deeper" is to align the final portfolio so that the artifact is on the left page and the commentary, explanation, and/or reflection is on the right page (see Figure 7.3). This mirror image allows the reader to review the artifact and then immediately see the thoughts of the person who included the entry.

Mirror Reflections

Artifact	Description
Criteria for a Speech	These are early criteria we created for our persuasive speeches. We watched three videos of speeches and then brainstormed the criteria for a good speech.
• Eye Contact	
• Organization	**Reflections**
• Content	
• Creativity	We tried to cover too many criteria for the first speech. We should have selected about five criteria to evaluate. The students had too much to think about and it was hard to finish the grading in five minutes.
• Appropriate Gestures	
• Visual Aid	
• Hook	

Figure 7.3

The reflective practitioner needs to conduct a self-assessment, a critical look at "how I am now" versus "how I would like to be."

Sometimes people prefer to separate the description of the entry from the reflection. The description section describes the entry (what it is, who developed it, why it is included, what the context of the piece was) and the reflection section features the reflections or reactions of the professional: "What have I learned from this piece? How can I connect it to other things? What do I still need to do?" Sometimes an entry is critical enough to warrant a whole page of description and reflection to document its importance.

Self-Evaluation

"To see ourselves as others see us." —Robert Burns

The reflective practitioner needs to conduct a self-assessment, a critical look at "how I am now" versus "how I would like to be." Even though few people enjoy hearing their own voices on tape or seeing themselves on video, these methods are valuable tools for identifying needed improvement (see Figure 7.4).

Evaluation of Video

Teacher: _Kathy Brown_   Date: _November 16_

Description of Class: This is a heterogeneous group of 35 eleventh-grade students enrolled in the American Literature course.

Description of Lesson

Unit: *Red Badge of Courage* (Civil War Unit)

Context: We had been discussing whether Henry, the protagonist, was a coward because he ran away his first time in battle.

Objective: To have students reflect on the terms "hero" and "coward" and apply them to their own lives.

Target Observation Area: I will observe how well I question students and elicit thoughtful responses. I want to probe for deeper understanding.

Hook: I asked for students' reactions to this quote: "Cowards die many times before their death; the valiant taste of death but once." *Julius Caesar,* Shakespeare

My Insights from Viewing the Tape: I would ask a question and then wait five to seven seconds before I called on a student. When Mike didn't have a response, I asked who his personal heroes were and then asked if he could name any "cowards." Once he answered these questions, he commented on the quote. I need to wait longer after the student answers to allow for additional answers or piggybacking from other students.

Signed: _Kathy Brown_   **Figure 7.4**

Administrators could tape their presentations at Back-to-School Night and analyze how well they explained ideas to parents. Did I talk too fast? Did I use educational jargon that confused parents? Was my speech too long? The administrator could include a copy of the video in the portfolio with an analysis of the speech and a reflection on what she could do to improve future presentations.

Counselors could use an audiocassette to record their facilitation of meetings in order to analyze their facilitation skills. Teachers could record on audiotape or videotape a lesson they teach and then review the tape and evaluate their effectiveness in meeting their objective. They could later include the video or cassette in their final portfolio with a critique of the experience, focusing on areas they want to improve. Educators could also include audio or video tapes of students giving a performance or creating a project as evidence that students are learning and the educators are achieving their target goals.

Transfer

"Ordinary learning contrasts with transfer. In ordinary learning, we just do more of the same thing in the same situation . . . Transfer means learning something in one context and applying it in another." (Fogarty, Perkins, and Barell 1992, ix)

Eisner has said that if it's not worth teaching, it's not worth teaching well. Teachers must ask themselves the critical questions, "Why am I teaching this? Does it have transfer potential? How can students use it in other situations?" Costa (as cited in Fogarty, Perkins, and Barell 1992, xii) suggests that teachers "selectively abandon" everything without transfer potential and "judiciously include" those things that have transfer power.

Just as students need to be able to "automatize" knowledge and skills in order to transfer them to other situations, so too educational professionals need to become more thoughtful and reflective in reaching their target goals in order to transfer them to other teaching situations. They need to seek generalizations, look for opportunities to apply prior knowledge, monitor their thinking, and ponder their strategies for approaching problems and tasks (Fogarty, Perkins, and Barell 1992).

Making the Connection

Many people have described "transfer" as the most important outcome of education. If students are *not* able to transfer what they have learned in school to real-life situations, what have they really learned? So too, if professionals implement a strategy or program in their classroom or school that few students ever use, what have they accomplished? To meet their focus goals, educators must incorporate mediation strategies that bridge learning into their teaching. Fogarty and Bellanca (1989) have suggested a strategy that promotes transfer (see Figure 7.5, page 98).

Metacognition and Transfer

The more practitioners take the time to reflect on their experiences, the more they will begin to make the connections between prior knowledge, current learnings, and future applications. Metacognitive reflection is a prerequisite to transfer. The more professionals think about their practices, share their insights with peers, and write about their reactions, the more they will clarify their thoughts and assess their ability to meet their target goals. Moreover, the reflection must be performed on a regular basis in order to be effective. Waiting until the last minute to write reflections for a whole year's worth of artifacts defeats the real purpose of the portfolio and weakens the link between metacognition and transfer.

Educational professionals need to become more thoughtful and reflective in reaching their target goals in order to transfer them to other teaching situations.

Transfer: The Creative Connection
Reflecting Metacognitively

Reflect on your transfer level by asking: Am I . . .

Ollie the Head-in-the-Sand Ostrich		Missing appropriate opportunities; overlooking; persisting in former ways?
Dan the Drilling Woodpecker		Performing the drill exactly as practiced; duplicating with no change; copying?
Laura the Look-Alike Penguin		Tailoring, but applying in similar situations; all looking alike; replicating?
Jonathan Livingston Seagull		More aware; integrating; subtly combining with other ideas and situations; using with raised consciousness?
Cathy the Carrier Pigeon		Carrying strategy to other content and into life situations; associating and mapping?
Samantha the Soaring Eagle		Innovating; taking ideas beyond the initial conception; risking; diverging?

(From Fogarty and Bellanca 1993, 300. Reprinted with permission.)

Figure 7.5

Metacognitive reflection is the most critical component of a professional portfolio. It allows reflective practitioners to review, analyze, and refine their teaching on an ongoing basis. Without reflections, portfolios are just "containers of stuff"; with reflections, portfolios constitute frameworks for professional growth.

Reflective Lesson Planner

Name: _Kathy Brown_   Grade: _11_   Date: _____

Topic: _Performance Rubric_   Lesson: _Introducing Students to Rubrics_

Describe what happened	Describe your feelings
Before the Lesson	Thoughts
I wrote a fun rubric assessing school lunches to model for the students.	I wanted students to be comfortable with the process and have fun before we created a real rubric.
During the Lesson	Strategies that work; lessons learned
I assigned roles for the group work. Two groups couldn't think of a topic and one group struggled with criteria and indicators.	Form groups to include a "creative" person in each group.
After the Lesson	Insights for future lessons
After each group shared their rubric, we talked about the process of developing rubrics. The fun rubric helped prepare them for the real rubric.	Do one fun rubric with the class to model before assigning groups to do them.

Reflective Stems

Create stem questions that trigger responses and provoke insight into what a person is thinking.

This piece gave me new insight into one of my students because . . .

I will save this piece forever because . . .

People who knew me ten years ago would not believe this piece because . . .

This piece shows I have met my target goal because . . .

This piece shows I have a great deal to learn about my topic because . . .

Portfolio Rejection Log

Name: _Kathy Brown_   Focus Topic: _Authentic Assessment_

Explain why you rejected items from your working portfolio.

Date	Rejected Item	Rejection Rationale
Sept. 1	First speech rubric	We tried to include too many criteria for the first speech. Also, we used a three-point scale with no zero.
Nov. 6	My rubric for the American Lit. research papers.	I realized that my "rubric" was really just point values for doing things with no regard for quality.
Dec. 9	The videotape of me teaching students how to create fun rubrics.	The camera was focused on me, but I wanted the students' reactions.

Self-Evaluation

Name: _Kathy Brown_

Focus Topic: _Authentic Assessment_

1. Describe the experience you are evaluating.
   I am introducing the fun rubric to my students.

2. Describe your method of self-evaluation.
   I had my peer videotape my lesson.

3. What do you feel you did well?
   I showed the students two fun rubrics for evaluating school lunches. They enjoyed them.

4. What would you do differently the next time?
   I would have modeled a fun rubric with the class before I assigned them to do one in groups. Some groups were really confused.

5. How can you improve?
   I need to practice creating more rubrics so I'll be confident leading my students through them.

Reflective Lesson Planner

Name: _____   Grade: _____   Date: _____
Topic: _____   Lesson: _____

Describe what happened in the lesson	Describe your feelings
Before the Lesson	Thoughts
During the Lesson	Strategies that work; lessons learned
After the Lesson	Insights for future lessons

Reflective Stems

Create stem questions that trigger responses and provoke insight into what a person is thinking.

1. This piece shows my professional growth because . . .

2. This piece will surprise (my principal, peers, students) because . . .

3. If I could reteach this lesson I would change _____ because . . .

4. I could never have included this piece (five, ten, twenty) years ago because . . .

5. This piece showed me that educational theory doesn't always translate into educational practice because . . .

Brainstorm additional stems:

6.

7.

8.

9.

10.

Portfolio Rejection Log

Name: _____   Focus Topic: _____

Explain why you rejected items from your working portfolio.

Date	Rejected Item	Rejection Rationale

Self-Evaluation

Name: _____   Focus Topic: _____

1. Describe the experience you are evaluating.

2. Describe your method of self-evaluation (videotape, cassette tape, photographs, script, other).

3. What do you feel you did well?

4. What would you do differently the next time?

5. How can you improve?

Reflections

 # Transfer Journal

After reviewing the "Transfer Birds" on page 98, which bird best represents your stage of development in achieving your professional goals?

I feel I am most like transfer bird _____ because . . .

Chapter 8

Teacher Evaluation

"For years educators have looked for alternatives to traditional evaluation practices, which are faulted for being both ineffective and injurious to teachers' self-respect. Evaluation strategies that rely on standardized checklists and other bureaucratic methods continue to be widely used even though they contribute little to teacher growth." (Smith and Scott 1990, 33)

The Case Against Traditional Teacher Evaluation

Every spring, teachers and administrators in schools throughout the country begin the ritual of the annual "teacher observation blitz." Principals and assistant principals, clipboards in hand, dart in and out of teachers' classrooms, observe for twenty to thirty minutes, script everything, and then rush back to the office to fill out their summative evaluation forms. These forms later become the focus of the administrator/teacher conference and, eventually, become a part of teachers permanent personnel records. Unfortunately, many teachers "play it safe" and conduct a sure-fire direct instruction lesson that fulfills all the requirements of the checklist.

Shanker (1996, 223) notes that most teachers are subjected to an evaluation process based on simplistic or unarticulated standards of best practice. Moreover, "these assessments are usually carried out by administrators who know little about exemplary teaching, and the process does little to ensure quality or to improve teaching practice."

Validity and Reliability of Teacher Observation Instruments

"Although on the surface, one might expect observation instruments to provide more valid assessments of teacher performance than paper and pencil tests, these forms of assessment also raise serious questions of both validity and reliability." (Gellman 1992, 39)

Gellman (1992, 40, 42) defines *validity* as "the question of whether a measurement instrument is, in fact, assessing that which we want to assess." She describes an acceptable level of *reliability* as one relying on the judgment of raters based on a common set of criteria on which to judge a set of products or performances. These terms are important because they are also critical issues in the evaluation of professional portfolios that are used to assess teacher performance.

Although there are some highly developed observation instruments, such as the North Carolina Teaching Appraisal Instrument (TPAI), according to Gellman (1992, 39), "most teacher observation instruments are highly informal." Soar, Medley, and Coker (1983, 39–40, as cited by Gellman) argue that assessment procedures should have four basic attributes:

The theory that current methods of observation are more valid and reliable than portfolio assessment is controversial.

1. They should present each individual being assessed with a standard task.

2. They should provide a record of performance.

3. They should have an agreed upon scoring key.

4. They should have publicly available standards against which an individual's performance can be measured.

Gellman argues that most traditional modes of teacher evaluation do not meet these criteria. Teachers are observed teaching a wide variety of lessons to a wide variety of students. Furthermore, the teaching behaviors being rated are vaguely defined and subject to wide interpretation and the subjective values of the observer. The fact that the observation is usually performed by a single supervisor on a single occasion provides a "snapshot" of one performance, but "it cannot indicate whether it is representative of the teacher's performance at other times in other classes or on other lessons" (Gellman 1992, 40). Moreover, even though there may be an agreed upon scoring key—poor, average, or outstanding—or a list of behaviors that are checked as "present" or "absent," "there tends to be little more than cursory attention given to assuring that these ratings have the same meaning for different raters. Furthermore, published norms are almost nonexistent."

The theory that current methods of observation are more valid and reliable than portfolio assessment, therefore, is controversial. Both types of assessment could be tainted if the scoring instrument does not measure what it is *supposed to measure* and does not measure it *consistently* and *reliably.* Moreover, it is essential that the evaluators in both types of assessment are trained to use the instruments.

Direct Instruction Model vs. Constructivist Model

Searfoss and Enz (1996) describe the frustration of a growing number of competent teachers who have embraced the constructivist philosophy of education. These teachers use discovery learning, cooperative student interactions, and thematic teaching only to have to "switch back" to a traditional direct instruction lesson for their end-of-the-year observation. They have to resort to this type of subterfuge because the checklist on the evaluation instrument does not reflect the holistic approaches they are using. In addition, "They reported feeling unappreciated and unvalued, even though their principals had rated them highly. Teachers also felt that they missed opportunities for meaningful feedback and collegial discussion about the complex pedagogy of their practice" (Searfoss and Enz 1996, 39). In other words, can an instrument be considered valid if it only measures one type of teaching—direct instruction?

Bernhardt (1994, 148–49) says, "Traditional teacher evaluations neither assess teamwork nor the context of the school in determining how well the individual has performed. They seldom ask the teacher to reflect on her or his performance in a meaningful way or to be analytical about student performance. As a consequence, traditional teacher evaluations often foster mediocrity, destroy motivation and self-esteem, and do not lead to improved personal performance." Traditional evaluation instruments also cause many teachers to "play the game." One master teacher with twelve years' teaching experience expressed her frustration:

Can an instrument be considered valid if it only measures one type of teaching— direct instruction?

> Tomorrow the principal will evaluate me. I will create a version of my best direct instruction lesson. My principal will love the lesson and rate my teaching performance as excellent. Unfortunately, the lesson she will see has almost nothing to do with the way I really teach or the way I believe children learn. (Searfoss and Enz 1996, 38)

The Purposes of Evaluation

According to Furtwengler (1992) and Rooney (1993) (as cited in Searfoss and Enz 1996, 38), teacher evaluation has traditionally served two unequal purposes:

1. The primary purpose has been to determine a teacher's suitability for continued employment.

2. The secondary purpose (and the one used most infrequently) is to provide teachers with feedback on performance to stimulate reflective thought.

Unfortunately, the secondary purpose of "providing constructive feedback"— not just check marks—has much less formal support in schools, even though it is the most valuable outcome of teacher evaluation, once the primary purpose has been met. Administrators who have little time to spare must concentrate on reviewing new teachers and recommending them for tenure and monitoring veteran teachers for problems. Regan (1993) says administrators are forced to choose where to spend limited time, and many administrators make the rational decision to devote their energies to beginners and other teachers whose competence is in question instead of spending time working with the competent teachers who want to grow professionally.

McGreal (as cited in Brandt 1996) urges school boards and state legislators to develop an "assistance track" for teachers who are having problems rather than design an entire evaluation system just for those one or two "bad eggs." He suggests instead building an evaluation system for the majority of teachers who are going to be there for life.

As Rand Corporation researchers Wise and Darling-Hammond (as cited in Smith and Scott 1990, 33) state, "Bureaucratic evaluation may be sufficient for monitoring whether the teacher is performing in a minimally adequate fashion, but it typically cannot assess higher levels of competence or deliver valued rewards or advice to most teachers."

Many administrators make the rational decision to devote their energies to beginners and teachers whose competence is in question instead of working with the competent teachers who want to grow professionally.

Performance-Based Evaluation

Glatthorn (1996, 59) notes several reservations about the practice of evaluating teachers solely on the basis of student achievement as measured by test results:

1. No authoritative tests exist in most areas of curriculum.

2. The use of test results is too susceptible to intentional distortion.

3. The practice elevates tests themselves to the level of curriculum goals.

4. No test can evaluate the difficulty of the teacher's task in the wide variety of work circumstances.

Because of the deficiencies of evaluating a professional solely on the basis of students' test scores, many educators choose to include student achievement as one important aspect of the evaluation process, but they combine it with goals, criteria, competencies, or professional standards as part of the total professional portfolio.

Goal-Based Evaluation

In a goal-based evaluation, supervisors assess performance by determining if and to what extent educators achieved the goals they establish in conjunction with the supervisor. An example of such a goal would be to have students improve their scientific problem-solving skills as measured by pre- and post-tests. This type of evaluation is similar to the informal professional development track. In this approach, it is necessary to clarify the role of the supervisor. In the professional development portfolio, with a focus on growth (not evaluations) the supervisor functions as a *supporter* who helps the educator develop as a professional but does not evaluate; the relationship is more like that in cognitive coaching. In goal-based evaluation, however, the supervisor acts both as a *coach* and as an *evaluator* who submits a summative evaluation of the teacher for the record. Glatthorn (1996) adapts McGreal's (1983) "practical goal-setting approach" to make it more compatible with the use of the portfolio (see Figure 8.1).

Goal-Based Evaluation

Step One: Administrator and Teacher Set Goal

Purpose: To review school goals, student achievement results, and teacher's prior performance.

Step Two: Teacher Presents Significant Learning-Focused Goal

Purpose: To focus on <u>one</u> significant goal for the year that would make a major difference in student growth and student achievement.

Step Three: Teacher Specifies Assessment Method

Purpose: To specify how progress toward the goal will be measured.

Step Four: Teacher States Methodology for Attaining Goal

Purpose: To develop methods that reflect a systematic analysis of what needs to be done.

Step Five: Teacher and Supervisor Agree on Resources

Purpose: To decide on funds, materials, time, and observational feedback needed. They agree on the number and purpose of classroom observations focused on goal-related activities.

(Adapted from Glatthorn 1996, 60–61)   **Figure 8.1**

In goal-based evaluation, classroom observations made by the supervisor focus only on goal-related classroom activities.

In goal-based evaluation, classroom observations made by the supervisor focus only on goal-related classroom activities. Also, teachers must specify how they will assess their success in meeting their goal. The assessment phase introduces an accountability factor that is not always present in the informal track of professional development portfolios. In addition, all the decisions agreed upon by the supervisor and the teacher should be finalized in a written professional development plan that both the supervisor and teacher sign. The plan becomes a part of the portfolio (see sample in Figure 8.2, page 110). Also included in the portfolio is *specific documentation* that each of the activities in the professional development plan has been completed. In this model the teacher includes a self-assessment indicating whether the teacher believed that the achievement of the goals was *satisfactory* or *more than satisfactory*. The final portfolio is reviewed by the administrator and examined and discussed by the administrator and the teacher at an end-of-the-year conference.

"Since it is assumed that the teacher's overall performance is satisfactory, the conference should emphasize reflection, with the administrator

The goal-based portfolio introduces the accountability factor that requires teachers to demonstrate that students are benefiting from the teacher's intervention.

Professional Development Plan

Learner-Focused Goal and Assessment Measure: Students will use performance rubrics to evaluate their own written work. A pre- and post-assessment will be used to measure results.

Signed: __Kathy Brown__   Signed: __Mr. Perry__   Date: __9/12__
(Teacher)   (Supervisor)

Action Plan	Documentation in Portfolio
1. Review research on creating rubrics.	• Fishbone synthesis of resources • Précis of key article • Interview with district assessment coordinator
2. Pre-test. Give students a copy of a descriptive paragraph they wrote and ask them to evaluate their work and assign a grade.	Results of their self-evaluations • Their comments and grades • My grades • Graph comparing grades
3. Develop rubrics.	Copies of the rubrics
4. Have rubrics critiqued by other English teachers and district assessment coordinator.	Copies of their critiques
5. Teach two lessons that incorporate rubrics with feedback from supervisor.	Edited videotape of lessons with my comments and a copy of supervisor feedback
6. Post-test. Give students a copy of their descriptive paragraphs and ask them to evaluate their work using a rubric.	Results of their self-evaluations • Their comments and grades • My grades • Graph comparing grades

Figure 8.2

asking questions that enable the teacher to think about the year in a meaningful and productive manner" (Glatthorn 1996, 63). At the end of the conference, the administrator submits a review of the reflective dialogue and the portfolio in a summative evaluation for the record.

The major difference between the professional development portfolio discussed in previous chapters and the goal-based portfolio is summarized in Figure 8.3. The goal-based portfolio introduces the accountability factor that requires teachers to demonstrate that students are benefiting from the teacher's intervention.

Schmoker (1996, 25–26) argues that when specific goals do not exist, one-shot staff development programs fill the void. Districts can report that the entire staff learned a new program and presume that this new practice or program will benefit the students. But the evidence is clear, he adds, that

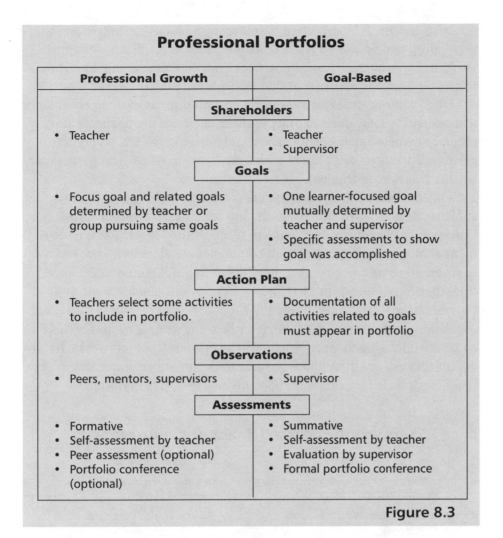

Professional Portfolios

Professional Growth	Goal-Based
Shareholders	
• Teacher	• Teacher • Supervisor
Goals	
• Focus goal and related goals determined by teacher or group pursuing same goals	• One learner-focused goal mutually determined by teacher and supervisor • Specific assessments to show goal was accomplished
Action Plan	
• Teachers select some activities to include in portfolio.	• Documentation of all activities related to goals must appear in portfolio
Observations	
• Peers, mentors, supervisors	• Supervisor
Assessments	
• Formative • Self-assessment by teacher • Peer assessment (optional) • Portfolio conference (optional)	• Summative • Self-assessment by teacher • Evaluation by supervisor • Formal portfolio conference

Figure 8.3

The goal-based portfolio provides documentation that student learning is the bottom line of professional development.

"most of what goes on in the name of innovation has a limited impact on student learning." The goal-based portfolio provides documentation that teachers are, in fact, producing measurable results with the new strategies, methodologies, and interventions and that student learning is the bottom line of professional development.

Criteria-Based Evaluations

Criteria-based evaluations are structured around specific criteria of effective teaching. Glatthorn (1996) says that this type of portfolio is used primarily by these organizations:

1. Schools of education to evaluate student teachers

2. School districts to evaluate teachers for tenure and contract renewal

3. Professional organizations to evaluate teachers for special licenses or certificates

Wheeler (1993, 4) states that "while many agencies are still in an exploratory or field-testing phase (e.g., professional certification of experienced teachers by the National Board for Professional Teaching Standards, beginning teaching licensure in Connecticut, the master teacher program in Texas), some agencies are now using portfolios for assessing performance and evaluating individuals in order to make decisions about successful program completion, licensure, hiring and job assignments, and other personnel decisions (e.g., career ladder programs in Arizona and Tennessee, teacher licensure in Oregon)."

Colleges of education often use criteria-based portfolios to evaluate student teachers. As mentioned in the Introduction, professors at the University of Memphis require student teachers to keep portfolios to document demographic data, placement conferences, and performance review in six areas, using a five-point scale: (1) planning, (2) communication, (3) leadership, (4) teaching strategies, (5) classroom management, and (6) evaluation (Chance and Rakes 1994, 1–3).

Perkins and Gelfer (1993, 236) describe some sample competencies that could document teacher performance in a portfolio (see Figure 8.4). Teachers collect evidence throughout the year to document their mastery of each criterion. It is also important to differentiate the level of performance for

It is important to differentiate the level of performance for novice teachers, veteran teachers, and teacher/leaders.

Samples of Expected Teacher Competencies

Content and Curriculum

- Activities promote problem solving, decision making, and creativity.
- Lessons are related to children's experiences.

Methodology and Classroom Organization

- Small groups in the classroom are flexible and related to the needs and interests of different students.
- Students are given opportunities to explore issues and concepts.

Planning

- Objectives are stated.
- Materials and equipment are listed.

Manages Classroom Instruction and Behavior

- Activities and teacher questions are sufficiently open-ended to allow creative and divergent thinking to occur.
- Teacher has establised a set of rules and procedures to prevent disruptive behavior.

Communicates Effectively

- Teacher is sensitive to needs and concerns of others.
- Teacher respects the rights of others.

Evaluates Students' Performance

- Teacher uses a variety of assessment and evaluation procedures.
- Teacher reports progress to parents.

Uses Appropriate Resources

- Media selections match learner variables.

Exhibits Professionalism

- Accepts constructive criticism and is willing to admit mistakes.
- Teacher is dedicated and enthusiastic.

Note: Levels of competencies can be indicated by designated code. For example, S represents satisfactory and N represents needs improvement.

(Perkins and Gelfer 1993, 236. Reprinted with permission.)

Figure 8.4

novice teachers, veteran teachers, and teacher/leaders. The evaluation scale could include criteria for each level to ensure that teachers are engaged in continuous improvement (see blackline master on page 128).

The portfolio should be structured according to the criteria, and it should include a wide variety of data sources such as videotapes, reflective essays, teacher work samples, official records, student evaluations, student feedback, student work, etc., relevant to the specified criteria or competencies. Many teachers are using technology to capture their documentation on computer disks.

Standards-Based Evaluation

The National Board for Professional Teaching Standards (NBPTS) was established in 1987 in response to a recommendation that the Carnegie Task Force on Teaching as a Profession put forth in *A Nation Prepared: Teachers for the 21st Century*. The National Board—a nonprofit organization governed by a 63-member board of directors, the majority of whom are teachers—sets standards for what accomplished teachers should know and be able to do and certifies teachers who meet those standards. Teachers who earn National Board Certification demonstrate through performance-based assessments that they

- Are committed to students and their learning.
- Know the subjects they teach and how to teach those subjects to students.
- Are responsible for managing and monitoring student learning.
- Think systematically about their practices and learn from experience.
- Are members of learning communities.

The Interstate New Teacher Assessment and Support Consortium (INTASC), created in 1987 as a program of the Council of Chief State School Officers, is engaged in a multistate effort to craft model licensing standards for teachers that reflect the intent of the standards for students. INTASC's primary constituency is state education agencies, including state departments of education and independent standards boards responsible for teacher preparation and licensing. Currently, thirty-six states are active in the INTASC projects. Also participating are members of the following organizations: the National Board of Professional Teaching Standards, the American Association of Colleges for Teacher Education, the National Council for Accreditation of Teacher Education, the National Association of State Boards of Education, the National Association of State Directors of Teacher Education and Certification, the National Education Association, and the American Federation of Teachers.

INTASC's approach to creating standards is based on a holistic conception of career development for teaching professionals. Thus, it aims not only to describe rigorous expectations for beginning teachers but also to lay out the elements of competent entry-level practice in a way that ensures consistency with accomplished teaching. In this way licensing standards describe the goals toward which teachers work throughout their careers to achieve excellence in their profession (Ambach 1996, 208). INTASC presented the standards in the form of ten principles (Figure 8.5), which have since been elaborated in terms of underlying knowledge, dispositions, and performance skills expected of all new teachers.

Teachers who are expected to meet such standards need to collect evidence in their portfolios to document their achievement of each standard.

INTASC's Ten Principles: Model Standards for Beginning Teacher Licensing and Development

- The teacher understands the central concepts, tools of inquiry, and structures of the discipline(s) he or she teaches and can create learning experiences that make these aspects of subject matter meaningful for students.

- The teacher understands how children learn and develop and can provide learning opportunities that support their intellectual, social, and personal development.

- The teacher understands how students differ in their approaches to learning and creates instructional opportunities that are adapted to diverse learners.

- The teacher understands and uses a variety of instructional strategies to encourage students' development of critical thinking, problem solving, and performance skills.

- The teacher uses an understanding of individual and group motivation and behavior to create a learning environment that encourages positive social interaction, active engagement in learning, and self-motivation.

- The teacher uses knowledge of effective verbal, nonverbal, and media communication techniques to foster active inquiry, collaboration, and supportive interaction in the classroom.

- The teacher plans instruction based on knowledge of subject matter, students, the community, and curriculum goals.

- The teacher understands and uses formal and informal assessment strategies to evaluate and ensure the continuous intellectual, social, and physical development of the learner.

- The teacher is a reflective practitioner who continually evaluates the effects of his or her choices and actions on others (students, parents, and other professionals in the learning community) and who actively seeks out opportunities to grow professionally.

- The teacher fosters relationships with school colleagues, parents, and agencies in the larger community to support students' learning and well-being.

Taken from The Interstate New Teacher Assessment and Support Consortium (INTASC) (Ambach 1996, 208. Reprinted with permission.)

Figure 8.5

Domains of Teaching Responsibility

Another method of teacher evaluation is described by Charlotte Danielson in *Enhancing Professional Practice: A Framework for Teaching* (1996). She describes how in 1987 the Educational Testing Service (ETS) began a large scale project to provide a framework for state and local agencies to use in making teaching licensing decisions. The PRAXIS Series includes Professional Assessments for Beginning Teachers and PRAXIS III: Classroom Performance Assessments for assessing teaching skills and classroom performance.

The complex activity of teaching is divided into four domains of teaching and twenty-two components clustered under each of the domains. The domains include: (1) planning and preparation, (2) the classroom environment, (3) instruction, and (4) professional responsibilities. The framework Danielson describes can be used with novice and veteran teachers for evaluation, but it also "offers the profession a means of communicating about excellence" (Danielson 1996, 5).

Critical Tasks

Another evaluation option related to criteria-based evaluation is allowing educators to identify the critical tasks in teaching specific subjects or in classroom management. Wolf (1991) describes how a group of teachers in the Teacher Assessment Project at Stanford achieved consensus about what is exemplary and essential in teaching elementary literacy after observing exemplary teachers, reviewing curriculum frameworks and research literature, and numerous discussions with teachers and researchers. They selected three diverse teaching areas for documentation in portfolios and then subdivided into them smaller, more manageable tasks—each of which became the basis for a portfolio entry:

Integrated language instruction

- Planning and adapting
- Teaching

Assessment of students

- Initial
- Ongoing
- Focused

Creating a literate environment

- Classroom design
- Adapting and using the environment

The final portfolio in elementary literacy was made up of entries for the seven tasks, along with an "open entry" in which each teacher included an area of special interest and a "background information entry" to describe the context in which they taught (Wolf 1991, 131).

Teachers developing portfolios might find it useful to meet in their cadres and go through a similar process to determine which critical tasks, competencies, or criteria would demonstrate an understanding of the essential and exemplary components in teaching a specific subject area.

Evaluation of Administrators

A consortium of twenty-four state agencies has drafted standards for administrators that can be used to evaluate their performance. Five of these states are now working with the Educational Testing Service (ETS) of Princeton, New Jersey, to create assessments for new principals based on the standards. In phase two, the states will work with ETS to come up with a model portfolio that could be used to evaluate school leaders.

The Interstate School Leaders Licensure Consortium developed the following "Draft Standards for School Leaders." In addition to the six standards displayed in Figure 8.6, the draft includes more than one hundred indicators that describe the knowledge, dispositions, and performances needed to meet the standards.

School systems and colleges are trying to align the purpose of the evaluation with the type to obtain the best results.

Draft Standards for School Leaders

A school administrator is an educational leader who promotes the success of all students by:

1. Facilitating the development, articulation, implementation, and stewardship of a vision of learning that is shared and supported by the school community.

2. Advocating, nurturing, and sustaining a school culture and instructional program conducive to student learning and staff professional growth.

3. Managing the organization, operations, and resources for a safe, efficient, and effective learning environment.

4. Collaborating with families and community members, responding to diverse community interests and needs, and mobilizing community resources.

5. Acting with integrity, fairness, and in an ethical manner.

6. Understanding, responding to, and influencing the larger political, social, economic, legal, and cultural context.

(Interstate School Leaders Licensure Consortium as cited in Olson 1996, 5)

Figure 8.6

School systems and colleges are experimenting with combinations of the types of evaluation described in this book, trying to align the purpose of the evaluation with the type to obtain the best results (see Figure 8.7).

Types of Evaluation and Portfolios

Administrative Time Commitment	Target Group	Type
Intensive	Pre-Service Teachers	**Criteria-Based Evaluations:** Professors of Education want to make sure future teachers are qualified in Instruction, Curriculum, Assessment, and Management
Intensive	Beginning Teachers (Non-Tenured)	**Criteria- or Competency-Based Evaluation:** Principals want to assure teacher competency in content, methodology, planning, management, communication, assessment, and professionalism using observations, videotapes, portfolios
Intensive	"Assistance Track" Teachers	**Competency-Based or Goal-Based Evaluation:** Principals meet with teachers having problems and develop a professional development plan directly related to the problem areas
Minimal Commitment (Informal observation, post-conferences)	Veteran Teachers (Tenured), Formative Evaluation	**Professional Development:** These teachers select their own focus goals. They work independently or in cadres.
Intensive (Pre-conference, formal observations,	Veteran Teachers (Tenured), Summative Evaluation	**Goal-Based Performance Evaluation:** Teachers meet individually with supervisor to prepare professional development plan. They are observed formally or informally and they complete a portfolio as part of their summative evaluation.

Figure 8.7

Assessing teacher performance with professional portfolios has many advantages over traditional observation, but it can also be very challenging.

The Challenge of Evaluating Portfolios

"Although many schools, districts, and teacher training institutions have started using portfolios, few have put extensive effort into developing solid scoring procedures. Scoring of portfolio materials is heavily dependent on the professional judgment of those doing the scoring. The need for clear performance criteria, scoring rubrics, benchmarks, and rating guidelines is critical." (Wheeler 1993, 10)

Assessing teacher performance with professional portfolios has many advantages over the traditional observation method, but it can also be very challenging. Since summative evaluation reports are used to promote, demote, retain, or dismiss personnel, the stakes are high. In fact, many people refer to formal portfolios as "high stakes portfolios" because they play such a critical part in the evaluation process.

Formative and Summative Evaluations

Formative evaluation is assessment that takes place *during* the developmental stages of a project or product. A teacher developing a portfolio for such evaluation can receive feedback from peers and supervisors that he can use to improve or revise his performance. The goal of a formative evaluation, therefore, is to provide ongoing dialogue and support to improve performance or product. In contrast, *summative* evaluation is defined as assessment of the overall effectiveness of a performance or product *after* it has been fully developed and implemented. A teacher's portfolio in this context is reviewed to judge overall teaching performance or to "sum up" the effectiveness of the teacher's success in meeting learner-centered goals, as well as to make personnel decisions.

Obviously, if the formative stages of portfolio development provide ongoing dialogue, collegial support, opportunities to revise, improve, and perfect one's performances and products, the summative stage will not be as critical. Moreover, the process of achieving the goal will become as important as the final product.

However, conducting a summative evaluation of a professional portfolio requires a great deal of thought, planning, and organization. If the evaluation is for purposes of administrative decision-making (personnel changes, tenure, dismissal), it is critical that the portfolio be used as only one component of the evaluation process. Glatthorn (1996, 64) warns that "Valid assessments use multiple measures: several observations of teaching performance; anecdotal records of performance of non-instructional duties; conferences; and analysis of such documents as lesson plans, tests, and student grades."

Wheeler (1993, 13) warns that schools and districts that want to use portfolios as part of the teacher evaluation process ". . . should proceed with caution. As a start, they should try using them for professional development and for encouraging teacher self-evaluation and reflection." Moving the professional portfolio from the low-stakes, informal, formative track to the high-stakes, formal, summative track requires a more structured approach to determine:

- Who will the shareholders or stakeholders be?
- What will be included?
- When will it be assessed?
- How will it be evaluated?
- How will the results be used?

In addition, Glatthorn (1996, 34) warns that portfolios also have a few drawbacks from the perspective of the supervisor and administrator: "Since the contents are assembled and presented by the teachers, they represent a

If evaluation is for purposes of administrative decision-making, it is critical that the portfolio be used as only one component of the evaluation process.

highly selective record of teaching. They cannot comprise the sum of objective evidence for evaluation, especially if issues of certification and tenure are involved."

Holistic and Analytical Evaluations

"Professional judgment may be the key to portfolio evaluation, but simply conjuring up the words does not solve the problem. In order for people to exercise such judgment in a disciplined manner, they need to be very clear about the performance criteria." (Wolf 1991, 135)

Scoring Terminology

According to Herman, Aschbacher, and Winters (1992), *criteria* for judging performance have been called many things—scoring criteria, scoring guidelines, rubrics, and scoring rubrics. Basically, all mean a *description of the dimensions* for judging performance, a *scale of values* for rating those dimensions, and the *standards* for judging performance.

"Criteria are necessary because they help you judge complex human performance in a reliable, fair, and valid manner. Scoring criteria guides your judgments and makes public to students, parents, and others the basis for these judgments." (Herman, Aschbacher, and Winters 1992, 45)

Portfolios can be scored *holistically,* where raters assign a single score based on the overall quality, or *analytically,* where raters give separate ratings to different aspects of the work. (Criteria incorporating several outcomes are analytic.) Herman, Aschbacher, and Winters (1992, 72) also state that two issues concerning scoring criteria for student portfolio assessment could also apply to professional portfolios:

1. What are the criteria for selecting the samples that go into the portfolios?

2. What are the criteria for judging the quality of the samples?

Other questions need to be addressed. How will progress be evaluated? How will different tasks, videos, art work, essays, journal entries and the like be compared or weighted in the assessment? What is the role of reflection in the assessment? Who will "judge" the portfolio?

It is imperative that all evaluators of portfolios be knowledgeable of the scoring methods and well trained in the model to ensure consistency in the ratings. Moreover, the evaluations need to be valid and reliable.

Scoring Process for Materials in Portfolios

Wheeler (1993, as cited in Burke 1996, 85) suggests it is important to address the scoring process when designing professional portfolios. Some of the issues include:

1. Whether each piece, selected pieces, combinations of pieces, or the total collection will be scored.

It is imperative that all evaluators of portfolios be knowledgeable of the scoring methods and well trained in the model.

2. Whether analytic, holistic, or a combination of scoring approaches will be used.

3. Who will be scoring and what training they will have received.

4. What scoring rubrics will be used to judge or grade each item, and who will develop them and select and/or prepare the benchmarks to go with them.

5. Who will monitor the judges and ensure the fairness, accuracy, and integrity of the scoring process.

6. What type of scale or system will be used to report the results of the portfolio scoring to the individual teacher and to others (e.g., mentor, teacher, evaluator).

Holistic Scoring

Researchers with the Teacher Assessment Project (TAP) at Stanford University spent four years exploring and developing new approaches to teacher evaluation. The resulting methods were intended to assist the National Board for Professional Teaching Standards in its creation of a voluntary certification of teachers for elementary and secondary schools.

Wolf (1991) had already noted that, since a portfolio contains much more information than is normally available for assessing a teacher's competence, each teacher's portfolio is unique because its contents have been customized to fit the teacher's personal teaching style and the context of his teaching situation. Consequently, the TAP team decided to evaluate portfolios holistically rather than use analytical scoring and take each portfolio apart for a point-by-point analysis. The evaluators used "professional judgment" to arrive at guidelines or criteria. Wolf had also observed, "Without some kind of structure or guidelines, people tend to go to one extreme or the other—either they retreat to unsubstantiated global impressions based on first reactions or gut feelings, or they try to simplify the assessment task by looking for specific, objective criteria and become overly narrow in their evaluation" (135). The trained examiners, experienced and knowledgeable in the content area and grade level, rated each portfolio according to the criteria of the National Board for Professional Teaching Standards (see page 113).

Holistic and Analytical Scoring

Another method of evaluating portfolios involves using both holistic and analytical scoring. Glatthorn (1996) describes how an evaluator should follow these steps:

Holistic

1. Assemble all portfolios to be evaluated.

2. Check each design to ensure that the portfolio meets minimum standards.

3. Return incomplete portfolios to the teachers for additional work.

Since a portfolio contains more information than is normally available for assessing a teacher's competence, each teacher's portfolio is unique because its contents have been customized to fit the teacher's personal teaching style.

4. Read carefully each portfolio that meets minimum standards (holistic review to gain a general impression of overall quality).

5. Sort portfolios into as many piles as there are rating levels (if a school district uses three levels—more than satisfactory, satisfactory, not satisfactory— there will be three piles).

6. Review all the portfolios again to ensure the first judgment is a valid one.

Analytical

7. Make an analytical rating of each portfolio.

8. Take each criterion, review the evidence, and give a rating for each.

9. Use the same rating terminology as in holistic scoring.

10. Give the final rating as an overall assessment of the general quality of performance—not as an average of the analytical ratings.

A holistic approach to portfolio evaluation does seem to enable teaching to be assessed more coherently than is possible in an analytic evaluation of separate skills or competencies. Regardless of the scoring method used, though, the impact of creating and sharing professional portfolios outweighs the concerns about holistic versus analytical scoring.

Portfolio Reviews

"Evaluation and tenure decisions often lack a tangible connection to a clear vision of high-quality teaching . . ." (Darling-Hammond 1996, 195)

The call to "judgment" in the professional portfolio process can be intimidating, threatening, or adversarial if not approached in the proper spirit. The traditional forms of performance review usually involve one supervisor reviewing the data and making a final evaluation in the form of a checklist, narrative review, or summative evaluation. Because of the size of some staffs and the demands on principals' time, some administrators or principals may not be familiar with the area of interest or goals selected by teachers. In the new spirit of collegiality, inviting people other than or in addition to the supervisor to review a portfolio offers a wide range of possibilities.

A Committee of Peers

One type of review could involve a small committee of peers selected by the person being evaluated. The teacher could select who would be on his committee, much as a doctoral candidate selects his dissertation committee. This idea is a radical departure from the one-on-one conference with the principal, but it could be very effective for the following reasons:

1. Committee members could be selected because they were the peer, mentor, or cognitive coaches who worked closely with the person.

2. Committee members could be experts in the goal area and, therefore, would know a great deal about the level of competencies or the

A holistic approach to portfolio evaluation does seem to enable teaching to be assessed more coherently than is possible in an analytic evaluation of separate skills or competencies.

quality of the documentation of a specific area. Members could be from another school or district, be a staff developer, or be a district resource person.

3. Committee members would be in a better position to judge the growth and development of a candidate for evaluation because they have monitored the journey towards the goals, criteria, competencies, or standards more closely.

4. A more equitable decision could be made by a committee discussing the merits of each portfolio as opposed to the final evaluation of one judge.

More than one teacher have expressed tremendous frustration and disappointment at discovering that the one person evaluating his or her portfolio knows very little about the topic *or* the entire portfolio process. As part of the coaching skills taught and used at each school, attention should be given to helping all staff members become a "committee of peers" to provide constructive feedback and fair evaluations of their fellow professionals.

Portfolios, in conjunction with other valid assessments, enable teachers to document their teaching in a way no other form of assessment can.

The End Result

Despite all the components that must be considered in the area of teacher and administrator evaluation, it is evident that portfolios, in conjunction with other valid assessments, enable teachers to document their teaching in a way no other form of assessment can. As Wolf (1991, 136) states, "Classroom observations allow teaching to be seen in context, but observations, which tend to take place only a few times a year, are isolated snapshots, disconnected from the events that preceded or followed the observed lesson." Bernhardt (1994, 149) recommends using teacher portfolios, peer coaching, and collaborative action research combined with self-assessment strategies as tools for nontraditional teacher evaluations. By restructuring the current evaluation process, everyone wins.

Given the complexity of teaching, goals at least provide a framework to guide educators on the pathway to excellence. As Danielson (1996, 7) states, "An important step to enhancing the stature of educators in the family of professions is defining clearly what constitutes excellence in teaching. As long as practitioners present teaching as a mysterious art form without well-defined duties and competencies, the larger community will regard it with some mistrust."

Examples

Self-Assessment of Goals

Name: _Kathy Brown_   Topic: _Performance Rubrics_

Major Goal: *Help students self-evaluate their own work.*

Subgoal:
Students will determine criteria for all work.

| Not Attempted 0 | Partially Achieved 1 | Mostly Achieved 2 | Totally Achieved (3) |

Comments: *We now take the time to brainstorm specific criteria for every assignment.*

Subgoal:
Students will create indicators of quality work.

| Not Attempted 0 | Partially Achieved 1 | Mostly Achieved (2) | Totally Achieved 3 |

Comments: *Some of our indicators are too vague. We need to be more precise in our language.*

Subgoal:
Students will develop rubrics to evaluate their own work.

| Not Attempted 0 | Partially Achieved 1 | Mostly Achieved (2) | Totally Achieved 3 |

Comments: *Some criteria such as creativity, originality, and understanding are difficult to measure.*

Goal-Based Evaluation

Goal: The students will improve their cooperative social skills as measured by observation checklists, number of verbal reprimands, and a student survey.

Comment on how your evidence documents attainment of your goal.

Observation Checklists
I used three types of checklists. One included the five social skills I targeted. The second was completed by groups to monitor their skills. The third was an individual checklist for each student.

Verbal Reprimands
The first week of the study, I averaged 6 verbal reprimands per hour of instruction. After ten weeks of teaching social skills along with my content. I gave verbal reprimands about once per hour.

Student Survey
The students felt the time spent teaching social skills—especially conflict resolution skills—were beneficial both inside and outside the classroom.

Overall Evaluation of Goal Attainment
I feel I have accomplished my goal of improving students' cooperative skills. Students can now work in groups to develop meaningful projects and performances without discipline problems.

Signed: _____ Date: _____

Self-Assessment of Critical Tasks

Classroom Climate	0 Not Yet	1 Attempted	2 Meets Expectations	3 Exceeds Expectations
• Room set-up				X
• Rules and consequences				X
• Expectations for behavior				X

Comments: *I spent a lot of time the first weeks of school developing rules and consequences with the student.*

Social Skills	0 Not Yet	1 Attempted	2 Meets Expectations	3 Exceeds Expectations
• Skills taught explicitly				X
• Assessment of social skills		X		

Comments: *I taught five social skills using the T-chart, but I didn't do a good job assessing students' use of the skills.*

Conflict Resolution	0 Not Yet	1 Attempted	2 Meets Expectations	3 Exceeds Expectations
• Proactive strategies			X	
• Effective interventions			X	
• Long-term follow-up		X		

Comments: *I need to develop more strategies to help students mediate their own conflicts.*

Scale: 20 - 24 = Exceeds
        14 - 19 = Meets
        8 - 13 = Attempted
        0 - 7 = Not Yet

Score: **18**

Professional Portfolio Self-Evaluation

Name: _Kathy Brown_ Topic: _Performance Rubrics_

1. What did you do well in achieving your goals?
   I involved all my students in the process of creating rubrics to assess our performances, projects, and portfolios.

2. What would you have done differently in achieving your goals and why?
   I would have collected more sample rubrics to use as models. It is much easier to "adapt" than to "create."

3. What recommendations could you make to others based on your findings?
   With the emphasis on accountability, teachers should work to make their evaluations more objective and fair. Rubrics help achieve objectivity.

4. Based on what you have learned, what future studies would you consider doing to help your students learn?
   I want to explore portfolios in more depth. I now see the value of having students see their growth and development over time.

Evaluation of Portfolio

Domain I: Planning and Preparation   Component 1f: Assessing Student Learning

LEVEL OF PERFORMANCE

ELEMENT	Unsatisfactory	Basic	Proficient	Distinguished
Congruence with Instructional Goals	Content and methods of assessment lack congruence with instructional goals.	Some of the instructional goals are assessed through the proposed approach, but many are not.	All the instructional goals are nominally assessed through the proposed plan, but the approach is more suitable to some goals than to others.	The proposed approach to assessment is completely congruent with the instructional goals, both in content and process.
Criteria and Standards	The proposed approach contains no clear criteria or standards.	Assessment criteria and standards have been developed, but they are either not clear or have not been clearly communicated to students.	Assessment criteria and standards are clear and have been clearly communicated to students.	Assessment criteria and standards are clear and have been clearly communicated to students. There is evidence that students contributed to the development of the criteria and standards.
Use for Planning	The assessment results affect planning for these students only minimally.	Teacher uses assessment results to plan for the class as a whole.	Teacher uses assessment results to plan for individuals and groups of students.	Students are aware of how they are meeting the established standards and participate in planning the next steps.

(Danielson 1996, 78. Reprinted with permission.)

Self-Assessment
of Goals

Name: _____ Topic: _____

Major Goal:

Subgoal:	Not Attempted 0	Partially Achieved 1	Mostly Achieved 2	Totally Achieved 3

Comments:

Subgoal:	Not Attempted 0	Partially Achieved 1	Mostly Achieved 2	Totally Achieved 3

Comments:

Subgoal:	Not Attempted 0	Partially Achieved 1	Mostly Achieved 2	Totally Achieved 3

Comments:

Subgoal:	Not Attempted 0	Partially Achieved 1	Mostly Achieved 2	Totally Achieved 3

Comments:

Goal-Based Evaluation

Comment on how your evidence documents attainment of your goal.

Goal: _____

Goal: _____

Goal: _____

Overall Evaluation:

Signed: _____ Date: _____

Self-Assessment of Critical Tasks

Classroom Climate	**0** **Not Yet**	**1** **Attempted**	**2** **Meets** **Expectations**	**3** **Exceeds** **Expectations**
• Room set-up				
• Rules and consequences				
• Expectations for behavior				
Comments:				

Social Skills	**0** **Not Yet**	**1** **Attempted**	**2** **Meets** **Expectations**	**3** **Exceeds** **Expectations**
• Skills taught explicitly				
• Assessment of social skills				
Comments:				

Conflict Resolution	**0** **Not Yet**	**1** **Attempted**	**2** **Meets** **Expectations**	**3** **Exceeds** **Expectations**
• Proactive strategies				
• Effective interventions				
• Long-term follow-up				
Comments:				

Scale:

Score:

Self-Assessment of Competencies

Data gathered through observations, interviews, and portfolio artifacts provide evidence that the educator does the following:

Competencies	0 Not Yet	1 Attempted	2 Meets Expectations	3 Exceeds Expectations
1. Understands the curriculum and the methodology				
2. Organizes the classroom effectively				
3. Plans interactive lessons to meet students' needs				
4. Manages students appropriately				
5. Communicates effectively to students and parents				
6. Assesses student work authentically				
7. Uses a variety of resources to enhance learning				
8. Demonstrates professionalism				

Comments:

Portfolio Rubric

Name _____ Date _____

☐ Self-Evaluation   ☐ Peer Evaluation   ☐ Supervisor Evaluation

CRITERIA	1 **Meets Some Requirements**	2 **Meets All Requirements**	3 **Exceeds Requirements**	SCORE
A. ORGANIZATION				
1. Completeness and Timeliness	Some entries missing or incomplete and/or submitted late	All entries completed according to directions; submitted on time	All entries completed and organized correctly	
2. Visual Appeal (cover, graphics artwork, layout)	Missing key element or elements; meets minimum standards	Key elements demonstrate originality	Key elements demonstrate creativity and style	
3. Format (spelling, punctuation, grammar, usage, typing)	Entries contain several errors	Entries are error-free	Entries demonstrate high level of writing skills	
Comments:				
B. EVIDENCE OF UNDERSTANDING				
1. Knowledge of Key Concepts	Entries reflect recall and comprehension	Entries reflect analysis and synthesis	Entries reflect evaluation and application	
2. Process	Entries reflect basic understanding of topic	Entries reflect high level of understanding	Entries reflect high level of understanding and transfer	
Comments:				

(Continued on next page)

© 1997 IRI/SkyLight Training and Publishing, Inc.

Portfolio Rubric (Continued)

CRITERIA	1 Meets Some Requirements	2 Meets All Requirements	3 Exceeds Requirements	SCORE
C. GROWTH AND DEVELOPMENT				
1. Group Interactions	Entries demonstrate minimum use of peer interaction	Entries demonstrate peer and group interactions	Entries demonstrate peer/cognitive coaching experiences	
2. Problem Solving	Entries demonstrate ability to identify problems	Entries demonstrate ability to brainstorm solutions	Entries demonstrate ability to implement creative solutions	
3. Goal Attainment	Some goals are not achieved	All goals are achieved	Some goals are exceeded	

Comments:

CRITERIA	1	2	3	SCORE
D. METACOGNITION				
1. Artifact Reflections	Reflections are missing or inappropriate	Reflections provide insight into teacher's thinking	Reflections provide evidence of insight and thoughtfulness	
2. Self-Assessment of Portfolio	Self-assessment is missing or lacks depth	Self-assessment reflects understanding of self	Self-assessment provides insight into professional growth	

Comments:

Comments:

SCORE _____

Reflections

Professional Portfolio Self-Evaluation

Name: _____ Topic: _____

1. What did you do well in achieving your goals?

2. What would you have done differently in achieving your goals and why?

3. What recommendations could you make to others based on your findings?

4. Based on what you have learned, what future studies would you consider doing to help your students learn?

Chapter 9

Conferences and Exhibitions

"A conference can be a wonderful opportunity to hear how students [educators] are thinking about their work. The quality of the conference is far more significant than the quantity of conferences." (Kallick 1992, as cited in Costa et al. 1992)

Portfolio Conferences

Kallick advocates that teachers use conferences to investigate students' attitudes toward their work. Her message also applies to administrators who need to discover teachers' attitudes toward their work. Principals face the same challenge that teachers face in their classes—finding time to talk individually with everyone they supervise. A principal with a faculty of 50–100 teachers is going to have to radically adjust her schedule to meet each staff member for a 20–30 minute conference once or twice a year to discuss professional development plans and final portfolios. The logistics of scheduling these conferences at the beginning and end of the school year challenge even the most dedicated administrator. Several reports from national commissions and educational experts, however, emphasize the critical role administrators will play in professional development and school change, despite the time constraints.

The Changing Role of School Leaders

The role of the school leader is changing. As reported by Olson (1996, 5), the National Policy Board for Educational Administration has included standards that specifically address teaching, learning, and professional growth. According to these standards, a school administrator is an educational leader who promotes the success of all students by

1. Facilitating the development, articulation, implementation, and

stewardship of a vision of learning that is shared and supported by the school community.

2. Advocating, nurturing, and sustaining a school culture and instructional program conducive to student learning and staff professional growth.

Olson further states that effective school leaders should have a deep understanding of teaching and learning—which the Board describes as the "heart and soul" of effective school leadership.

In addition, a 151-page report from the National Commission on Teaching and America's Future, entitled *What Matters Most: Teaching for America's Future,* proposes that by 2006 every student in America be provided with what it calls a new birthright—a competent, caring, and qualified teacher. The report states, "Our society can no longer accept the hit-or-miss hiring, sink-or-swim induction, trial-and-error teaching, and take-it-or-leave-it professional development it has tolerated in the past" (as cited in Bradley 1996b, 14). The Commission has urged action in five areas: setting high standards for teaching; reinventing preparation programs and professional development; overhauling recruitment; crafting policies to reward teachers' knowledge and skills; and creating schools that are structured so that students and teachers can succeed.

As part of the policy to reward teachers' knowledge and skills, school leaders will have a major role in determining salary incentives for teachers. They will also be involved in determining the criteria for evaluating their knowledge and skills. The professional development plan, the professional portfolio, and the final conference will, therefore, be critical to a teacher's summative evaluation, which, in turn, could determine tenure, promotion, licensure, professional certification, or salary incentive.

The principal, despite all the demands on her time to handle school management, will have to meet with teachers on a regular basis to plan, monitor, and evaluate the professional development plan and the professional portfolio. Policymakers are making school leaders responsible for assuring that teachers meet high standards and are "armed with the knowledge and skills that will help students reach ambitious academic goals" (Bradley 1996b, 14).

Effective school leaders should have a deep understanding of teaching and learning—the "heart and soul" of effective school leadership.

One-on-One Conference with the Principal

Beginning of the Year

Ideally, each teacher would meet individually with the principal for about thirty minutes at least twice a year to discuss professional development. Currently, most teachers meet once with the principal toward the end of the year to discuss the yearly observation and the summative evaluation form that both the principal and teacher must sign before submission to the district office.

Conferences could be requested by either the principal or the teacher, and they could be formal or informal, depending upon the type of professional development plan and the purpose for the conference.

The first conference could take place in the fall with each teacher meeting the principal to discuss her goals for the upcoming year and to finalize the activities and means of assessment for the professional development plan. For beginning teachers and for teachers new to the school or content area, the principal may discuss the competencies or criteria that are required for all nontenured staff members.

For the veteran "assistance track" teacher that the principal and other supervisors believe is not performing to standards, the principal might discuss with the teacher ways to improve performance in areas such as planning, knowledge of curriculum, teaching methodologies, classroom management, or professional interactions. They would then develop an improvement plan, discuss ways to assess the results, and set up observations and follow-up conferences.

Veteran teachers who have already demonstrated their mastery of teaching competencies could meet with the principal to decide on their focus goals for the coming year. Each teacher and the principal could develop a professional development plan to explore the topic selected and, in the case of formal evaluations, discuss the types of observations, visitations, and assessment tools to measure the teachers' success in achieving the goals.

Conference Questions for Principals to Ask Teachers
Beginning-of-Year-Conference Questions

1. What were your greatest successes with students last year?
2. What were some of your greatest challenges?
3. What areas do you want to work on for this year?
4. How will your interest in this area help your students?
5. What goals will you address this year?
6. What action plan do you have to achieve these goals?
7. How will you know whether you have been successful?
8. What help do you need from me (resources, observations, support)?

Throughout the Year

Principals can meet with all teachers to discuss problems, progress reports in reaching goals, classroom observations, or revisions in the professional development plan. These conferences could be requested by either the principal or the teacher, and they could be formal or informal, depending upon the type of professional development plan and the purpose for the conference.

Mid-Year Conference Questions

1. How are you doing in following your professional development plan?
2. Would you like me to get class coverage so your peer coach can observe you?

3. Would you like me to observe you?

4. Have you been meeting with your peer coach or cadre to reflect on your professional growth?

5. Do you want to observe teachers in other schools or attend workshops or conferences?

6. Are you on target to meet your goals?

End of the Year

The last conference of the year is usually devoted to discussing the results of the goals listed on the professional development plan and reviewing the documentation and reflections in the professional portfolio. These conferences are usually the most formal and in most cases the longest because the principal and the teacher will be discussing the effectiveness of the intervention, conclusions, and recommendations for follow-up studies. If the professional development plan and portfolio are parts of the formal evaluation, the teacher will need to fill out a self-assessment form and the principal will also fill out a form using the official evaluation instrument decided upon by the two of them or the standardized form used by all teachers in the school or district.

The last conference of the year is devoted to discussing the goals listed on the professional development plan and reviewing the documentation and reflections.

End-of-the-Year-Conference Questions

1. Show me how you have achieved your goal.

2. How have your efforts improved student achievement?

3. What evidence in your portfolio shows the results of your study?

4. What do you think you did well in your study?

5. If you could do something differently, what would it be?

6. What did you learn about yourself as an educator from this experience?

7. What new goals have you set?

Figure 9.1 illustrates a goal-focused summative evaluation conference.

Summative Evaluation Conference

Teacher: Kathy Brown   Principal: Mr. Perry

Principal: Let's review the professional development plan you and I wrote on September 12. Your goal was to help your students evaluate their own work using rubrics. Why did you select that goal?

Kathy: I was getting discouraged grading my students' writing assignments. They were making the same mistakes over and over. Their writing was not improving. Frankly, I was spending too much time correcting their papers. I wanted them to be more responsible for their own learning and to take pride in their work.

Continued on next page

IRI/SkyLight Training and Publishing, Inc.

Principal: How did you get interested in rubrics?

Kathy: I attended a workshop on authentic assessment last year. The presenter talked about the importance of criteria and of having students involved in establishing criteria for their own work. I read articles about authentic assessment. I watched the ASCD video series on Performance Assessment. I was hooked.

Principal: In your professional development plan you said you would give a pretest to the students to see how they could evaluate a narrative paragraph. How did your students do?

Kathy: Not very well. I graded their paragraphs, and in many cases, my grade was lower than the grades they gave themselves. Their comments showed that they were judging their papers on basic criteria such as spelling, grammar, and punctuation. They rarely addressed content, organization, or creativity.

Principal: I see that you included in your portfolio some of the fun rubrics you and your students developed. Tell me how that went.

Kathy: Well, it went pretty well. We started by doing a fun rubric to assess school lunches so the students would understand the process of creating rubrics. We used criteria like taste, smell, visual appeal, nutritional value, and cost. The rubrics were hysterical, and they got the kids excited about composing real rubrics.

Principal: I observed one of your classes when you developed a rubric to assess a descriptive paragraph with your students. How do you think the lesson went?

Kathy: I was really nervous because usually I have created the evaluation already. I told the students they were going to become a part of the process. We brainstormed criteria and voted on the indicators. The class argued a lot about what made a "4" rating, but we finally reached consensus.

Principal: I viewed a videotape of another lesson where your department chairperson observed. Tell me about that lesson.

Kathy: You'll see in my portfolio I included the videotape of that lesson and my reflection. The lesson involved the class revising the original rubric for the descriptive paragraph, because the students found the indicators too vague when they were using the rubric. I was happy that they saw the need to clarify their criteria and use more specific language.

Principal: I see in your portfolio you have the results of the posttest you gave to see if students improved their self-evaluation skills. Did your results turn out as you expected or were you surprised?

Kathy: For the posttest I asked the students to evaluate another narrative paragraph that they had written in class. This time, many developed a rubric before they assessed their work. As you can see on the comment section of the results, most used very specific terminology when discussing their work. The graph shows that 90% of the students gave themselves the same grade I gave them—that compared to only 70% during the pretest.

Continued on next page

IRI/SkyLight Training and Publishing, Inc.

Principal: What new goals do you want to work on for next year?

Kathy: I want to continue working on assessment because the students now see the value of creating rubrics for all our work. My next step is to incorporate portfolios as a means to collect and organize their work and reflect on their learnings. After completing my own portfolio, I see the value of talking about work with others.

Principal: I really enjoyed reviewing your portfolio and visiting your class. On the basis of my observation, your final portfolio and our conferences throughout the year, I am giving you a rating of Above Satisfactory, the highest rating. I've included comments on the form that you should read.

Kathy: Thank you for your comments and for your support through the year. I really appreciate that you got people to cover classes so my peer coaches could observe me. I also want to thank you for letting me visit English teachers at other schools who were using rubrics.

Principal: We've scheduled some time at the last faculty meeting of this year and we're devoting one of our inservice days in August for staff members to share the results of their studies. I know several teachers have expressed an interest in studying rubrics next year, so they will appreciate any advice you can give them.

Figure 9.1

Group conferences provide a great opportunity for colleagues to discuss the results of their research, the methods they would recommend to others, and educational issues affecting their students.

Group Conference with Principal

As mentioned earlier, a principal with a staff of fifty or more might have a difficult time meeting individually with each staff member at the beginning of the year to finalize the professional development plan and then again at the end of the year to review the success of the plan and/or the final portfolio.

One alternative to individual meetings is to meet with a group of teachers. Often several teachers decide to work together to pursue the same goal; therefore, the principal can meet with the group and discuss members' collective and individual progress. For instance, the principal could meet with the team that researched block scheduling or with the team that developed interdisciplinary units. The conference could be either informal or formal, depending on whether the conference would be considered part of the official evaluation or a culminating experience for professional growth.

Group conferences provide a great opportunity for colleagues to discuss the results of their research, the methods they would recommend to others, and educational issues affecting their students. One teacher involved in a conference on adopting school-wide portfolios remarked that it was stimulating to discuss such substantive issues when meeting with the principal and the teachers who were studying portfolios. She said, "Usually we only meet at traditional faculty meetings to discuss lunch and bus duty schedules and field trip guidelines. That's important—but having time to conference about educational issues is also important."

Even though the principal plays a major role in conferencing, other people can also play integral roles. Conferences are more effective if they are conducted on a regular and ongoing basis. Therefore, educators should consider several other communication options.

Other Conference Options

Peer Conferences

The whole professional development plan and professional portfolio process is more effective if each teacher pairs with a peer at the very beginning. This peer or "critical friend" is the person who shares the artifacts, reflects on the portfolio and on the journals, offers advice, and celebrates success throughout the journey. The peer also could be the peer coach who observes the partner in the classroom and/or videotapes lessons and helps critique them.

The peer is someone who usually teaches the same grade level or subject matter so she can help with content and methodology. It is critical to the portfolio process that at least *one* person shares the experience with the portfolio creator from the beginning to the end of the process.

Cadre Conferences

In many action research projects, teachers work on the same topic in groups of three to five. So too, cadres could form to study the same topic or problem because they have the same interests. In spring faculty meetings, groups often form to pursue similar interests—for example, a group of science teachers wants to study problem-based learning or a group of third-grade teachers wants to implement cooperative learning strategies to reduce behavior problems. These groups review the research and often devise similar action plans for the following year. It is only natural that group members meet regularly to discuss new findings, new directions, and new interventions. Group members also coach, observe each other's classes, and conduct conferences regularly to discuss professional development plans and the artifacts in their portfolios.

Mentor Conferences

Beginning teachers are often assigned mentors "to shepherd" them through the critical first three years of teaching. In the next ten years, about two million new teachers will enter the profession because of enrollment growth for students and the retirement of teachers. Retention of new teachers is low. As many as thirty to fifty percent leave within three to five years. The National Commission on Teaching and America's Future believes that the

It is critical to the portfolio process that at least one person shares the experience with the portfolio creator from the beginning to the end of the process.

high attrition rate is attributable to new teachers having no mentoring from experienced teachers. Mentors assigned to help new teachers could conduct conferences on a regular basis to help clarify the beginning teacher's goals. Often, novice teachers are required to submit criteria-based portfolios that cover a wide range of competencies ranging from planning to classroom management. The mentor can meet with the new teacher on a regular basis to model good teaching, share valuable insights, and discuss any problems the beginning teacher may be having.

Cognitive Coach Conference

"It cannot be overstressed that cognitive coaching is a non-evaluative peer coaching model." (Garmston 1992, as cited in Harp 1994)

Cognitive coaching provides a collegial relationship that supports teachers in becoming critically reflective about their work. It usually includes a preconference, a lesson observation, and a postconference.

In the *preconference* the peer coach invites the teacher to (1) elaborate on student learning goals, (2) describe how the teacher will know what the students are learning during a lesson, and (3) identify areas in which the peer coach can gather objective data for the teacher. Garmston (1992, as cited in Harp 1994) says, "The peer coach thus becomes another set of eyes for the teacher and a mediator of the teacher's processing of his or her own teaching experience."

During the *lesson* the peer coach collects only information about student learning and the data the teacher requested during the preconference. Such observations may focus on student performance, on-task behavior, wait time, questioning strategies, proximity, movement, a particular student's behavior, transitions between activities, or clarity of directions.

The *postconference* usually begins with an open-ended question such as "How do you feel the lesson went?" This type of question invites teachers to begin self-assessment. Garmston suggests the next question could be "What are you recalling from the lesson that's leading you to those inferences?" This type of question focuses on "monitoring and recalling what happened during a lesson"—an important cognitive function of teaching. Next, the teacher may be asked to think about some strategies or techniques that would have produced different results. Finally, the teacher is asked to project and apply what has been learned for future lessons.

Cognitive coaching's main goal is to help teachers modify their own and their students' behaviors by reflecting on what happened in the lesson. Data collection is fundamental to their self-analysis and self-coaching, but the processing of the lesson enables teachers to analyze the experience. Cognitive coaches, therefore, play a critical role in a teacher's professional growth. These pre- and post-conferences scheduled throughout the year promote cognitive and metacognitive reflection and help teachers accomplish their goals.

Mentors assigned to help new teachers could conduct conferences on a regular basis to help clarify the beginning teacher's goals.

Grade Level and Department Conferences

A teacher can select anyone at the school or district level to become her peer or cognitive coach. School counselors, psychologists, or media specialists are often called upon to assist teachers because of their expertise in certain areas and their availability to observe classes. Many teachers, however, select someone in their department, grade level, or interdisciplinary team to be their coach because this person also knows the specific content and strategies for dealing with students at different grade levels.

Often teachers bemoan the fact that they don't have enough time to talk with teachers who teach similar subjects to discuss new ways to approach the content. Such conferences about new directions in science, language arts, physical education, or new reading and writing strategies can be shared at regularly scheduled conferences throughout the year. Teachers can bring portfolio artifacts to reflect upon and discuss with fellow experts in their field.

Supervisor Conference

A supervisor can be a lead teacher, a department chair, a district coordinator, an assistant principal, a dean of students, a staff developer, or a team leader. If the teacher is on the professional growth track and completing a portfolio that is not part of an official evaluation, the supervisor would conduct informal conferences to share the portfolio. The purpose of the informal conferences would be to discuss the teacher's progress in meeting her goal and to review the artifacts in the portfolio and discuss the teacher's reflections and future goals.

If, however, the teacher's professional development plan and the final portfolio are parts of the yearly evaluation process, the conference becomes more formal. Moreover, the supervisor assumes the role of an evaluator and the results of the observations, conferences, and the portfolio process are summarized in an official summative evaluation that becomes part of the teacher's personnel file.

If the teacher's professional development plan and the final portfolio are parts of the yearly evaluation process, the conference becomes more formal.

Exhibitions

"The term [exhibition] hails from the eighteenth century and refers to an ubiquitous feature of the early American academies and common schools of the era. The exhibition, as practiced then, was an occasion of public inspection when some substantial portion of the school's constituency might show up to hear students recite, declaim, or otherwise perform. The point was to satisfy their constituency that the year's public funds or tuitions had been well spent now that some cohort of young scholars was now ready to move on or out" (McDonald et al. 1993, 2).

The Coalition of Essential Schools established by Theodore Sizer in 1984 at Brown University began with a charter group of twelve schools. The

Coalition is dedicated to exploring new systems of schooling for the twenty-first century and is guided by a set of common principles—one of which is that graduation from high school be based on genuine achievement rather than just putting in time. People still want to know what students can do as a result of their schooling. Exhibitions show that students have a genuine understanding in essential intellectual matters that they can apply in new contexts—not just scholastic knowledge.

For teachers, the National Commission on Teaching and America's Future recommends that states create professional standards boards to set rigorous requirements for teaching and "license teachers based on their demonstrated knowledge and skills rather than accumulated coursework" (Bradley 1996b, 15).

The final professional portfolio, a completed professional development plan, videotaped lessons, and records of observation all demonstrate a teacher's knowledge and skills, not just "school time." The professional community of educators shares new ideas and findings on a regular basis in educational publications, seminars, conferences, and workshops. Why not add an exhibition to the end of school events where faculty members can share the findings of their studies, review each other's portfolios and artifacts, and engage in active and meaningful conversations about education?

Portfolio Exhibition

In addition to showcasing new ideas and portfolios, exhibitions also encourage collegiality among departments, grade levels, whole schools, or districts. Each educator would bring her portfolio and leave it on one of several tables in a room. The portfolios could be clustered around topics, grade levels, or departments, so people could select groups that interest them. Each educator could prepare copies of a one-page abstract to highlight the study. People could take the abstract to read later and use as a reference in case they would like more information on a topic or might need a peer or mentor in case they want to pursue the same goal. The exhibition could be scheduled after school or at night, and members of the district staff, school board, and community could be invited to share the celebration.

Presentations

In addition to the portfolio exhibition, educators are often called upon either individually or in cadres to present their studies to faculty members or parent groups. These presentations can be considered professional staff development because, instead of hiring an outside expert to conduct an inservice, the "in-house experts" can share their expertise with their own faculty.

Long-Term Staff Development

Many schools call upon their own staff to train other staff members. For example, if Kathy Brown and her peers spend a year studying rubrics, they may be encouraged to share their experiences, insights, and examples with

The final professional portfolio, a completed professional development plan, videotaped lessons, and records of observation all demonstrate a teacher's knowledge and skills.

other teachers who are interested. Long-term transfer of new ideas is made possible if someone on staff is available to support teachers who need help in developing and sustaining the new ideas.

A Community of Learners

Darling-Hammond (1988, 59, as cited in Lieberman) talks about the new reform that suggests greater regulation of teachers, "ensuring their competence through more rigorous preparation, certification, and selection—in exchange for the deregulation of teaching—fewer rules prescribing what is to be taught, when, and how." She says, in essence, that all professionals make a bargain with society. The profession guarantees the competence of its members in exchange for the privilege of professional control over work structure and standards of practice. Society has to trust teachers to make the right decisions before it gives up regulating education through legislative mandates.

Teachers can earn their professionalism by demonstrating their competence in professional development plans, professional portfolios, and exhibitions of their work. Portfolios enable teachers to document their teaching to show the relationship between teaching and learning, and to show how they as professionals make decisions and solve problems with their community of learners. As Wolf (1991, 136) states, "Portfolios can give teachers a purpose and framework for preserving and sharing their work, provide occasions for mentoring and collegial interactions, and stimulate teachers to reflect on their own work and on the act of teaching."

Change is never easy. Educators must believe that despite all the extra work involved, they will grow as professionals as a result of this process. They must believe that the public will treat them as professionals and allow them to make decisions without interference. They must believe that their students will benefit from their expertise. They must believe that professional development is a lifelong process and that they play the most critical role in all of public education. As Sykes (1996, 465) has stated, "Teacher learning must be the heart of any effort to improve education in our society."

Teachers can earn their professionalism by demonstrating their competence in professional development plans, professional portfolios, and exhibitions of their work.

Examples

Conference with Principal

Questions that could be asked by the principal:

1. What were your goals this year?

2. Why did you select these goals?

3. What baseline data did you gather at the beginning of your study?

4. What were the results of your study?

5. What surprised you about the portfolio process?

6. How do you think you did meeting your goals?

7. What new goals are you planning to set?

Conference with Peer

Questions that could be asked by the peer:

1. How important was it for you to have a peer involved in this professional development process?

2. Did you feel concerned that one of your fellow teachers would be observing you several times during the year? Why or why not?

3. What was the most helpful thing I did for you this year?

4. Upon reflection, is there anything else I could have done to help you?

5. How did you feel about the feedback I gave after each observation?

6. Would you want to continue using the peer coaching next year? Why or why not?

Conference with Cadre Members

Questions that could be asked by the cadre:

1. Was it worth it to work as a team to achieve the goals?

2. What are the benefits of working as a cadre?

3. What are the problems of working as a cadre?

4. What impact did our study have on our students and the entire school?

5. What surprised us through the study?

6. If we conducted this study again, what would we do differently?

7. How does working together as a group compare to working alone?

Exhibition Ideas

1. Exhibit professional portfolios at a faculty meeting. Cluster portfolios by goals, topics, departments, or grade level. Review and discuss displayed portfolios.

2. Prepare a one-page abstract of the studies for distribution prior to displaying the portfolios.

3. Ask faculty volunteers to prepare a slide or computer demonstration of their portfolio to show at a faculty meeting or parent night.

4. Throughout the year, call upon one or two faculty members to share their portfolios at regularly scheduled meetings.

5. Have departments meet to share their portfolios.

6. Team up with another school to share portfolios.

7. Hold a district-wide exhibition to share portfolios.

Conference Questions

Brainstorm some thoughtful questions that could be asked during a conference about professional development plans and professional portfolios.

Question:

Question:

Question:

Question:

Question:

Exhibition Ideas

Brainstorm three scenarios where faculty members and administrators could share their portfolios and discuss their studies with each other, parents, and members of the community.

Reflections

Describe how the portfolio process has helped you grow as a professional.

_____
_____
_____
_____
_____
_____
_____
_____
_____
_____

What is your next step toward professional improvement?

_____
_____
_____
_____
_____
_____
_____
_____
_____
_____
_____

Share your final reflections with a peer.

Signed: _____ Peer: _____ Date: _____

Sample Portfolio

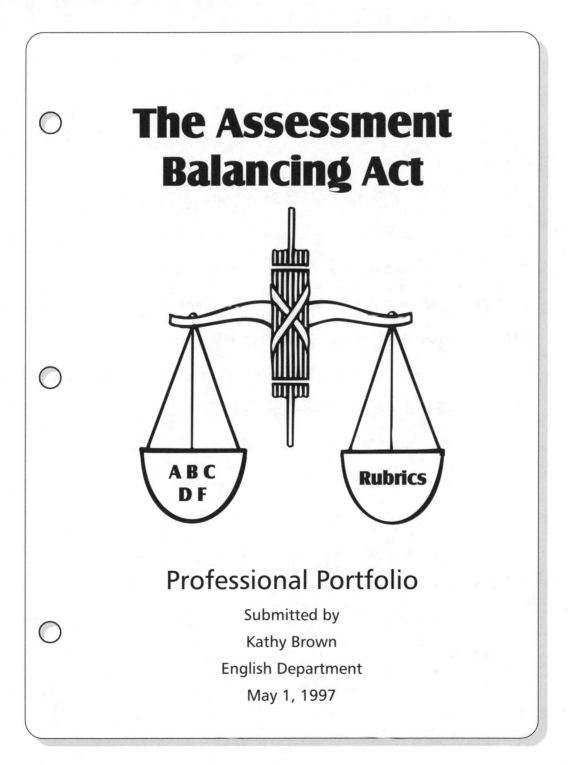

The Assessment Balancing Act

A B C
D F

Rubrics

Professional Portfolio

Submitted by

Kathy Brown

English Department

May 1, 1997

Contents

IRI/SkyLight Training and Publishing, Inc.

A Letter to My Readers

My cover depicts my goal of trying to balance the traditional assessments that students and parents recognize and expect (standardized tests, teacher-made tests, and report cards) with the newer, more authentic assessments that involve students in the evaluation process. I've labeled this process "The Assessment Balancing Act" because I'm trying to maintain a balance by integrating performance rubrics into my teaching so that my students will internalize the criteria and improve the quality of their projects and performances.

This portfolio represents the journey I started at the beginning of this year. Teamed with two other teachers in my department, we set the goal of having our students evaluate their own work using rubrics they created. I have included artifacts from both my students and myself, along with reflections about what I have learned.

Thank you for sharing my discoveries, reflections, and insights.

Kathy Brown
May 1, 1997

1

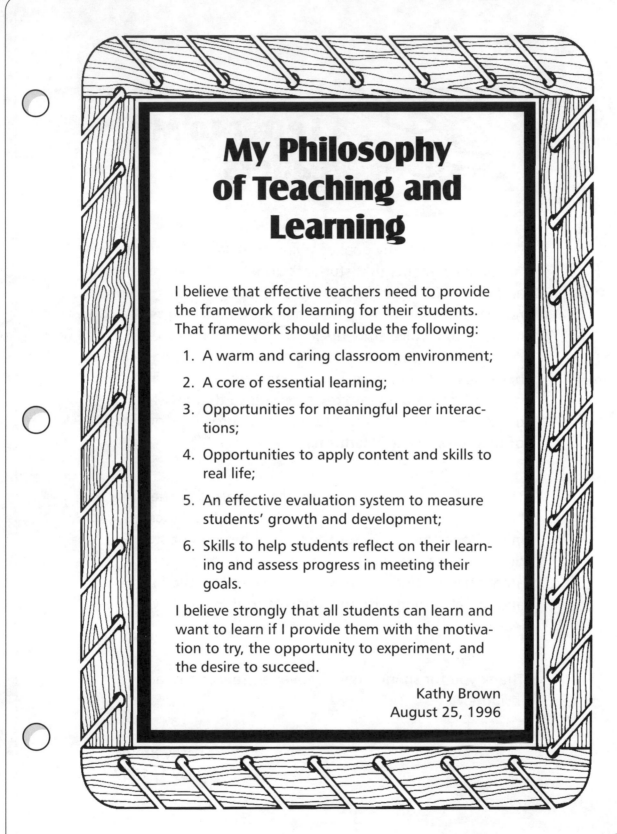

My Philosophy of Teaching and Learning

I believe that effective teachers need to provide the framework for learning for their students. That framework should include the following:

1. A warm and caring classroom environment;

2. A core of essential learning;

3. Opportunities for meaningful peer interactions;

4. Opportunities to apply content and skills to real life;

5. An effective evaluation system to measure students' growth and development;

6. Skills to help students reflect on their learning and assess progress in meeting their goals.

I believe strongly that all students can learn and want to learn if I provide them with the motivation to try, the opportunity to experiment, and the desire to succeed.

Kathy Brown
August 25, 1996

IRI/SkyLight Training and Publishing, Inc.

My Professional Development Plan

Name: ___Kathy Brown___ Date: ___August 1996___

Time frame for Plan: ___August 1996–May 1997___

Topic Selected: ___Student Self-Evaluation Using Performance Rubrics___

Rationale for Selecting Topic:

I am frustrated by the amount of time I spend grading my students' work, because in spite of my corrections, they make the same mistakes over and over. I want them to be responsible for their own learning and evaluate their work using performance rubrics that they help create. I hope that their learning will be more meaningful if they are part of the assessment process.

Team Members Involved:

Two English teachers in my department, Lois Moss and Patsy Angel, who share my frustrations and concerns about the grading process.

Essential Question:

Will my students learn how to evaluate their own work if we work together to develop the criteria and indicators in scoring rubrics that can help students assess their own papers, projects, and performances?

Related Questions:

1. Will rubrics help us be more consistent in our own grading?
2. Will students be able to generate criteria to evaluate their work?
3. How does traditional grading compare to rubrics?
4. Will rubrics improve the quality of the students' work?
5. Will rubrics help students reflect on their own learning and evaluate their own work?

Baseline Data:

I will collect samples of students' self-evaluations of their papers and their speeches in September to see how accurately they assess their work. I will compare the grades they gave themselves

3

to the grades I gave them. I will also ask the students to reflect on their work and list their strategies and weaknesses as writers and speakers.

Action Plan (Intervention):

I plan to teach students how to develop performance rubrics for evaluation of the quality of written work and oral presentations.

My Professional Goals:

1. Review literature and resources on the topic.
2. Work with other English teachers to create student rubrics.
3. Develop a professional portfolio reflecting on my growth in assessment.

Student-Centered Goals:

1. Students will develop effective performance rubrics.
2. Students will reflect on their learning.
3. Students will evaluate their work accurately and fairly.

Documentation:

1. Lists of available resources.
2. Sample rubrics created by my cadre of English teachers.
3. My portfolio to share with colleagues and supervisors.
4. Copies of rubrics developed by students.
5. Sample reflections written by students about their learning.
6. Self-evaluations completed by students.

Observations:

1. Two by peer.
2. One self-evaluation (video).
3. One observation by supervisor.

Conferencing:

1. Peer conferencing through the year.
2. Conference with principal at end of year.

4

IRI/SkyLight Training and Publishing, Inc.

Resource Review

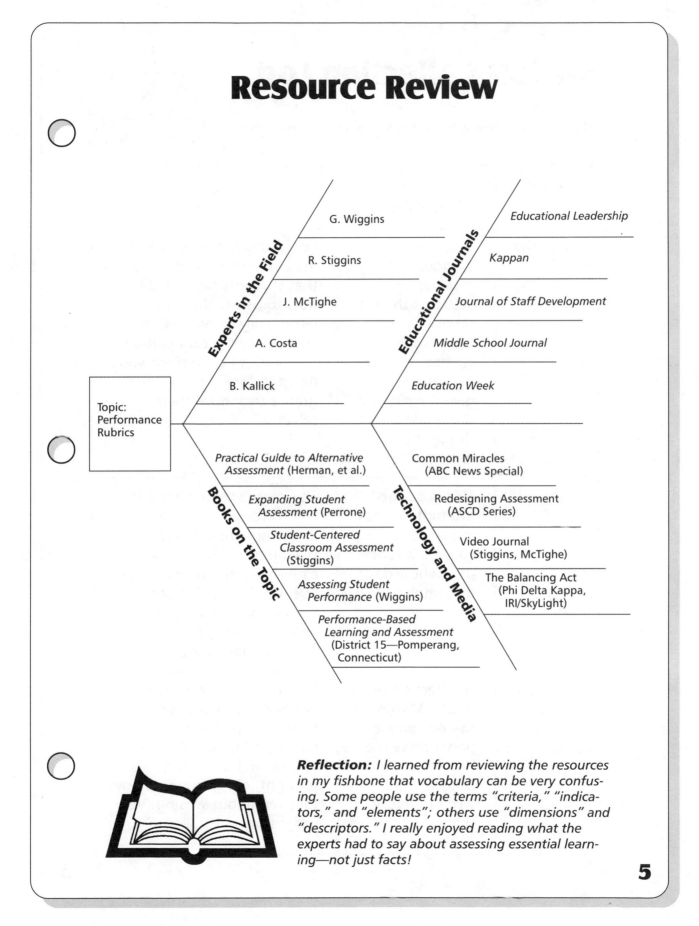

Topic:
Performance
Rubrics

Experts in the Field

G. Wiggins

R. Stiggins

J. McTighe

A. Costa

B. Kallick

Educational Journals

Educational Leadership

Kappan

Journal of Staff Development

Middle School Journal

Education Week

Books on the Topic

Practical Guide to Alternative
Assessment (Herman, et al.)

Expanding Student
Assessment (Perrone)

Student-Centered
Classroom Assessment
(Stiggins)

Assessing Student
Performance (Wiggins)

Performance-Based
Learning and Assessment
(District 15—Pomperang,
Connecticut)

Technology and Media

Common Miracles
(ABC News Special)

Redesigning Assessment
(ASCD Series)

Video Journal
(Stiggins, McTighe)

The Balancing Act
(Phi Delta Kappa,
IRI/SkyLight)

Reflection: *I learned from reviewing the resources in my fishbone that vocabulary can be very confusing. Some people use the terms "criteria," "indicators," and "elements"; others use "dimensions" and "descriptors." I really enjoyed reading what the experts had to say about assessing essential learning—not just facts!*

5

Artifact Collection Log

(These are three things I collected for my working portfolio)

Date	Item Collected	Rationale for Including in Portfolio
September 12	Results of a diagnostic assessment given students the first school week. I asked them to write a narrative paragraph then give themselves the grade they thought they deserved.	I used this piece as part of my baseline data to show that students had no idea how to assess their own work. They knew neither criteria nor my expectations. The grades I gave them were much different from the grades they gave themselves.
October 5	This is our first attempt at creating a rubric for a speech. It took us a whole day to complete.	This piece shows how difficult it was to decide on important criteria. We revised it after one use because we left out criteria on "Delivery"! We also added a "0" on the scoring guide and changed some of our imprecise language.
February 20	A reflection from Bobby Mason on the persuasive paper he wrote. He wrote that he used to hate writing before this year.	I would not have known about Bobby's conversion from hating to loving writing if I hadn't read his reflection. I had never thought to ask students how they *felt* about writing. Very insightful!

6

IRI/SkyLight Training and Publishing, Inc.

Classroom Artifact #1
First Speech Rubric (October 6)

Student: _____   Course: _____   Grade: _____

Performance to be assessed: __**Persuasive Speech**_____

1. CRITERION: _____**Organization of Speech**_____

   SCALE   1 ————————— 2 ————————— 3

ELEMENTS	INDICATORS			SCORE
a. Introduction	Hook that introduces topic	Hook that grabs our attention	Hook that electrifies us	____
b. Transitions	Choppy connections	Words/phrases to link ideas	Smooth/seamless transitions	____
c. Conclusion	Just stopped talking	Referred back to introduction	Powerful quote or question	____

2. CRITERION: _____**Content of Speech**_____

   SCALE   1 ————————— 2 ————————— 3

ELEMENTS	INDICATORS			SCORE
a. Research	Few sources cited	Some sources cited	Many key sources cited	____
b. Examples	Few examples to prove point	Some examples to prove point	Many relevant examples	____
c. Quotes	Few quotes	Some quotes	Many quotes	____

3. CRITERION: _____**Visual Aids for Speech**_____

   SCALE   1 ————————— 2 ————————— 3

ELEMENTS	INDICATORS			SCORE
a. Graphics	Minimal or no graphics	Colorful graphics	Colorful/creative graphics	____
b. Appeal	Little visual appeal	Captures our attention	Visually stimulating	____
c. Relevance	Minimal relationship to topic	Relates specifically to topic	Relates/reinforces topic	____

Reflection: *This is the first rubric created by the students. It was very difficult. We realized after we used it that we left out a whole section on Delivery (eye-contact, gestures, voice projection, etc.) We also didn't include a "0" in the scoring guide, so some students received 1 point even if they did nothing. We revised the rubric to make it more comprehensive and precise. We all learned from this experience. Notice how much improved our revised speech rubric is on the next page.*

7

IRI/SkyLight Training and Publishing, Inc.

Classroom Artifact #2
Revised Speech Rubric (October 25)

Performance Task: _Students will present a five-minute persuasive speech._

Goal/Standard: _Speak effectively using language appropriate to the situation and audience._

SCALE ⟍ CRITERIA	0 Not Yet	1 Student Council Elections	2 The Senate Floor	3 Presidential Debates
ORGANIZATION				
• Hook	None	Introduces topic	Grabs attention	Electrifies audience
• Transitions	None	Uses words to link ideas	Makes key connections between ideas	Smooth flow of ideas
• Closure	None	Lacks interest	Referred to introduction	Powerful and dramatic
CONTENT				
• Accuracy	3 or more factual errors	2 factual errors	1 factual error	All information is correct
• Documentation	No sources cited	1 source cited	2 sources cited	3 or more sources cited
• Quotations	No quotes	1 quote to support case	2 quotes to support case	3 key quotes to prove case
DELIVERY				
• Eye Contact	Reads speech	Looks at some people some of the time	Looks at some people all of the time	Looks at all of the people all of the time
• Volume	Could not be heard	Could be heard by people in front	Could be heard by most people	Could be heard by all people
• Gestures	None	Used a few gestures	Used some gestures appropriately	Used many appropriate gestures effectively
VISUAL AID				
• Graphics	None	Minimal	Colorful	Creative graphics that enhance speech
• Appeal	None	Little visual appeal	Captures our attention	Visually stimulates audience
• Relevance	None	Minimal relationship to topic	Relates specifically to topic	Relates and reinforces topic

Reflection: _At first I resented taking so much class time to work on the rubrics. I felt guilty because I was taking time away from course content. I then realized that our thinking about the criteria for giving a speech and our deciding on what makes a quality speech **was** the content. "Less is more," and even though I won't be able to "cover as much material" as usual, I feel I am doing a better job on the material I do cover. I just have to practice "Selective Abandonment" with my huge curriculum!_

8

Classroom Artifact #3
Student Journal Entry

I have this tremendous fear that I will get to college and never pass Composition 101. My brother took the course three times before finally giving up and dropping out of college. He told me about how picky college teachers are and about how much they "bleed" all over the papers with red ink.

Until this semester, I never made higher than a "C" on any paper. When I would get my paper back, I never knew what I could do to improve. Teachers wrote "Awk" next to sentences, but I didn't know what to do about it. After working with rubrics and doing peer editing, I now know specifically what is wrong with my papers. I like working with a target rather than playing Russian Roulette every time I turn in a paper.

Signed: __Pam Roberts__

Grade: __11th Grade__

Date: __March 13, 1997__

Reflection: *This journal entry really moved me because I had no idea this student felt like this about her writing. I also never knew how much she enjoyed peer editing. The students take peer editing seriously when they have a rubric to guide them. I hope Pam gains confidence in her writing before she gets to college.*

9

Classroom Artifact #4
Pictures of Students Working

This picture shows a group working on creating a rubric for their research paper. They had an easy time deciding how to evaluate spelling; they had a difficult time evaluating "understanding of key concepts."

I never realized how effective peer editing could be when rubrics are used. Students take their jobs very seriously. Here, Regina and Patty edit each other's narrative papers. The rubric gives them focus and makes the feedback much more specific and useful.

Reflection: When I first started teaching twenty years ago, I attended a writing workshop that dealt with peer grading. I tried it and it was a total disaster. Students gave all their friends an "A" because they didn't want to be unpopular. Kids would get off task and talk about the game Friday night instead of thesis statements. I abandoned the practice and returned to grading everything myself. Rubrics have made peer evaluations more effective because students have guidelines and can be more conscientious with their grades and more specific with the feedback they provide. I also like the way peer evaluations have helped "bond" my students. They seem to trust and respect each other more.

10

Classroom Artifact #5
Students' Self-Evaluations

September	March
Item: Narrative Paper	**Item:** Narrative Paper
Grade I should get: A	**Grade I should get:** B
Rationale: I believe I deserve an "A" because I wrote two whole pages and I tried as hard as I could. The story about my worst day of school was funny and interesting.	**Rationale:** I deserve a "B" on my story about my first plane ride because I didn't have enough dialogue. I also didn't use enough description, and I had two run-on sentences and one comma splice!
Tom P.	Tom P.

September	March
Item: Persuasive Speech	**Item:** Persuasive Speech
Grade I should get: C	**Grade I should get:** B
Rationale: I didn't know we were supposed to have a visual aid for the speech. (I must have been absent when you told us.) I also went two minutes over-time, but I didn't know we lost points for that.	**Rationale:** I followed the rubric guidelines about the time limits, the visual aid, gestures, eye contact, organization, etc. The only thing I didn't do well on was my documentation. I didn't give sources for my statistics and quotes.
Martin R.	Martin R.

*Reflection: The one thing I have always hated about teaching is giving grades. Kids say, "Why did you give me a 'C'?" "What is it that **you** want?" "What do we have to do to get an 'A'?" Now my students and I both know the expectations BEFORE the assignment. And, since they usually create the grading scale with me, they take responsibility for following the guidelines. Now they may get a "C," but they know it's not because the teacher hates them but because they didn't meet the standards.*

11

Classroom Artifact #6
Rubric for Letters to the Editor

My juniors created this rubric to evaluate the Letters to the Editor they had to write about a controversial issue.

Criteria	Indicators	1 Rejected by Church Bulletin Committee	2 Published in High School Newspaper	3 Published in Local Newspaper	4 Published in New York Times	Score
Quality of Information	• Accuracy	3 or more factual errors	2 factual errors	1 factual errors	All information is accurate	___ x 5 = ___ (20)
Persuasiveness	• Convincing arguments • Concrete examples	Faulty logic No examples	Some logic 1 example	Logical arguments 2 examples	Logical and convincing arguments	___ x 5 = ___ (20)
Organization	• Thesis statement • Support sentences • Conclusion	Missing 2 elements	Missing 1 element—lacks clarity	All elements included—clear focus	All elements enhance "flow" of letter	___ x 5 = ___ (20)
Written Style	• Grammar • Sentence Structure • Transitions	4 or more errors—lacks style	2–3 errors—choppy style	1 error—smooth style	No errors—fluid style	___ x 5 = ___ (20)
Mechanics	• Capitalization • Punctuation • Spelling	4 or more errors	2–3 errors	1 error	100% accuracy	___ x 5 = ___ (20)

Comments:

SCALE
A = 93–100
B = 86–92
C = 78–85
D = 70–77

Final Score: _____
(100)

Final Grade: _____

Reflection: The students and their parents were having a difficult time translating a rubric score to our traditional grading scale. They would have a score of 16 on a rubric, but they could not explain how they got an "A." Therefore, they devised a rubric that translated into a 100 point score. After we created this rubric, we decided that some criteria were more important than others and should be "weighted" to count more. We later created a weighted rubric for our portfolio. The parents really liked the specificity of the rubrics.

12

Teacher Artifact #1
Peer Response

Name: Kathy Brown   Peer: Lois Moss

Your Reactions	Peer Response
Select *one* artifact you have collected for your professional portfolio. (Describe it.) *A journal entry from one of my juniors, Pam R. (see page 9).*	What have you learned about this teacher from her description of the artifact? *Kathy seems moved by her students' frank comments about writing. Maybe the rubrics will give the students the confidence they need, both in high school and college. Kathy is genuinely concerned about the affective as well as the cognitive side of learning.*
How does this artifact demonstrate you are helping your students? *Pam is an average student who is easily frustrated. Her journal shows that she wants to be a good writer, but she never knew how to break the skills into specifics. The rubrics have helped her focus on specifics and evaluate her own work. Most students want the teacher's comments instead of comments from their peers.*	
What have you learned about yourself as a professional as you reflect on this artifact? *I re-read my philosophy of teaching and learning statement in the front of my portfolio. I really believe every student wants to learn and is capable of learning. Fear of failure (embarrassment, low grades, flunking out) keeps many students from trying. I'm glad I can give Pam the confidence to succeed.*	What comments or suggestions could you offer? *I think Kathy should spend even more time teaching students how to peer edit their papers using rubrics. Pam seems comfortable helping others and getting help. I would suggest ensuring the students work well together before pairing because some students resent feedback from their peers.*
Signed: ____Kathy Brown____ Date: ____March 20____	Signed: ____Lois Moss____ Position: ____English Teacher____ Date: ____March 25____

13

Teacher Artifact #2
Evaluation of Videotape
(Videotape included in portfolio)

Name: __Kathy Brown__   Focus Goal: __Students learn how to self-evaluate__

Lesson: __Writing Reflections__   Date: __November 8__

1. Describe the experience you are evaluating.
I introduced the process of writing reflections. I told the students I expected them to write a reflection on everything they do in my English course.

2. Describe your method of self-evaluation (videotape, cassette, photographs, script).
My friend Lois videotaped the 30-minute lesson for me.

3. What did you do well in this lesson?
The hook I used was to read the students some of the reflections I had written for my professional portfolio. They couldn't believe I was putting together a portfolio and writing about them!

4. If you could teach this lesson again, what would you do differently?
I would read them some reflections from other students so they could identify more with students' thoughts, but I didn't have any. I also would give them some stems like "The best thing I like about this . . ." to get them started.

5. How can you improve?
I need to get a copy of a book on portfolios that lists about 25 stem questions that motivate students to think and to write.

6. What advice have you received from your peers?
My friend Lois says I should ask the students to write reflections and then share some of them with a partner. They are usually too embarrassed to share them with the whole class. She also suggested that I ask for volunteers to share with the whole class.

14

Teacher Artifact #3
Cognitive Coaching Planner

Name: _____Kathy Brown_____   Peer Coach: _____Lois Moss_____

Phase One: Planning Conference (Date: October 6)

1. Lesson goal: To guide students in developing a rubric to assess their persuasive speeches.

2. Anticipated Teaching Strategies: Direct Instruction, Brainstorming, Cooperative groups, Voting.

3. Data to be Collected on Student Achievement: Scores students receive on final speeches using rubrics compared to scores received on earlier speeches not using rubrics.

4. Data the Coach Is to Collect:

   • Student involvement in process (number of students on task)

   • Questions teacher asks to elicit criteria for speeches

   • Group interactions when small groups are brainstorming criteria

   • Amount of time spent in writing rubric

Phase Two: The Lesson (Coach gathers data)

   • 28 of the 32 students in class were on task 100% of the time

   • Questions teacher asked:

   a. What qualities do you look for in a good speech?

   b. How many criteria can be effectively assessed in five minutes?

   c. Is this the most precise wording we could use?

   • Group Interactions: 2 groups were off track—weak leadership.

   • Time needed to write rubric: 55 minutes (the whole period)

Phase Three: Reflecting (Teacher shares impressions and critiques the lesson using data)

Kathy: — I forgot to assign group roles. That's why some groups didn't have leadership—no one assumed the role.

   — I should have shown several videos of speeches before I asked, "What qualities do you look for in a good speech?"

   — It took too long to arrive at consensus about the criteria.

Phase Four: Application Phase (Coach has the teacher identify teacher learnings and implications for future lessons).

Kathy: I need to assign roles and time limits for group work to assure on-task behavior. Since it takes so long to arrive at consensus, I should assign each group one criterion for homework. Their job would be to write a rubric to share the next day. It's easier to revise than to create in class.

15

Results of Study

I compared the students' self-evaluations of their narrative paragraphs made in September to the ones they made in March. I also compared the grades they gave themselves to the grades I gave them. The self-evaluations they made early in the school year were vague, general, and often inaccurate. It was evident that the students did not know what specific criteria to evaluate or how to judge the quality of the work. They also gave themselves higher grades than I gave them (their grades agreed with mine 70% of the time).

I asked the students to evaluate another of their narrative paragraphs in March after creating rubrics and working on self-evaluation techniques. The post-test showed that students were more descriptive, more reflective, and more aware of the critical attributes of their work. They also gave themselves more accurate grades (closer to mine) because they knew the criteria for evaluation. They were all more consistent and reliable in their grading. Moreoever, the grades they gave themselves agreed with the grades I gave them 90% of the time.

Implications

Students can be trained to evaluate their own work accurately and fairly if they create rubrics and if they work with peers (or individually) to analyze their work according to predetermined criteria and standards of excellence.

Recommendations

I believe all teachers should create performance rubrics to become more fair and consistent in the grading process. Rubrics focus on important outcomes—not just the skills that are easy to measure. I also recommend that teachers teach their students how to create and use rubrics.

16

IRI/SkyLight Training and Publishing, Inc.

Self-Evaluation of Goals

Name: __Kathy Brown__   Topic: __Performance Rubrics__   Date: __May 1997__

Goals	Not Attempted	Partially Achieved	Mostly Achieved
Professional Goals			
1. Review the literature and resources on topic			I have read 4 books, 5 articles, and viewed 4 sets of videos.
2. Work with other teachers to create rubrics		Three of us tried to create a rubric for research papers. It's hard to come to consensus.	
3. Develop a professional portfolio to reflect on my growth in assessment			I think I did a good job on my portfolio. It was time consuming, but I learned about myself.
Comments: I am embarrassed to admit that I have not kept up with my professional readings. Once I finished my Master's Program twelve years ago, I quit subscribing to journals and attending workshops. I am proud that I have become an Action Researcher about Assessment.			
Student-Centered Goals			
1. Students will be able to develop effective performance rubrics			The students now demand a rubric for every major assignment. They are becoming more precise in their language.
2. Students will be able to reflect on their own learning		Some students are very metacognitive in their reflections. Others write a few lines. We need to work on reflections.	
3. Students will be able to evaluate their own work accurately			Most students can evaluate their own work and set goals for themselves.
Comments: I've learned that just telling students "to reflect" isn't enough. We need to spend more time sharing and modeling reflections that are insightful. The stems help some students who have "writer's block."			

17

My New Professional Goals

Short-Term Goals
(By next Fall)

I want to work on writing more thoughtful reflections in my portfolio, rather than just describe what I did.

I would like to organize a district conference, "A Rubric Fair," for all the English teachers to share what we've created.

I want to work with other English teachers to create rubrics we all can use to grade book reports, research papers, exhibitions, etc. We need to be more consistent at our school.

Long-Term Goals
(The end of next year)

Now that I feel comfortable with rubrics, I'm ready to tackle more portfolios for my students. I realize how powerful portfolios can be.

New technology that is available for portfolios is something I would like to explore. Some teachers are creating electronic portfolios.

My assessments need to be more creative. I want to study Gardner's theory of multiple intelligences so I can include a repertoire of assessments—not just verbal or written work.

Kathy Brown

Reflection: I have always loved teaching, but it has always been an isolated profession. Teachers always talk in the workroom and at lunch, but our topics usually revolve around student problems or personal experiences. It's rewarding to discuss curriculum and instructional strategies with my fellow professionals. I was afraid at first, but I really love having my peers observe my classes and discuss my portfolio. I feel I am growing as a professional, and, most importantly, I'm energized by all the new things I am trying.

18

IRI/SkyLight Training and Publishing, Inc.

My Final Thoughts

When I studied Ernest Hemingway in graduate school, I read that Hemingway's prose was just the "tip of the iceberg" and one had to look below the surface to discover the real meaning. I feel that my one-year journey to help students evaluate their own work has been very successful; yet, I have just grazed the surface.

The more I learn, the more I realize how much *more* I need to learn. I've discoverd the following needs:

1. To refine my cooperative learning techniques to help students interact more effectively.

2. To learn more about student portfolios so I can organize a system for my 135 students.

3. To integrate technology into my assignments. I've seen the excitement of students when they use HyperCard to create multimedia performances and portfolios.

4. To include more of the multiple intelligences in my instructional methods, assignments, and assessments. English teachers tend to emphasize the *verbal/linguistic* too much.

My students love rubrics and they use them to assess their own work very critically. I've learned how much I enjoy working with my peers and sharing ideas. I've been teaching for twenty years, and I've just touched the "tip of the iceberg" of my professional potential.

19

Bibliography

ABC News 1993. *Common miracles* video.

Association for Supervision and Curriculum Development. 1991. *Redesigning assessment* video series. Alexandria, Va.

Costa, A. L., and B. Kallick. 1992. Reassessing assessment. In A. L. Costa, J. A. Bellanca, and R. Fogarty, eds. *If minds matter: A foreword to the future,* vol. II. Arlington Heights, Ill.: IRI/SkyLight Training and Publishing, Inc.

Educator in Connecticut's Pomperang Regional School District. 1996. *A teacher's guide to performance-based learning and assessment.* Alexandria, Va.: Association for Supervision and Curriculum Development.

Herman, J. L., P. R. Aschbacher, and L. Winters. 1992. *A practical guide to alternative assessment.* Alexandria, Va.: Association for Supervision and Curriculum Development.

McTighe, J., and F. T. Lyman. 1992. Mind tools for matters of the mind. In A. L. Costa, J. A. Bellanca, and R. Fogarty, eds. *If minds matter: A foreword to the future,* vol. II. Arlington Heights, Ill.: IRI/SkyLight Training and Publishing, Inc.

Miller, W. H. 1995. *Alternative assessment techniques for reading and writing.* West Nyack, N.Y.: The Center for Applied Research in Education.

Perrone, V., ed. 1991. *Expanding student assessment.* Alexandria, Va.: Association for Supervision and Curriculum Development.

Stiggins, R. J. 1994. *Student-centered classroom assessment.* New York, N.Y.: Macmillan.

Wiggins, G. 1993. *Assessing student performance: Exploring the purposes and limits of testing.* San Francisco, Calif.: Jossey-Bass.

20

Bibliography

Ackerman, R., P. Maslin-Ostrowski, and C. Christensen. 1996. Case stories: Telling tales about school. *Educational Leadership* 53 (6): 12–16.

Ambach, G. 1996. Standards for teachers: Potential for improving practice. *Phi Delta Kappan* 78 (3): 207–10.

Andres, T. E., and S. Barnes. 1990. Assessment of teaching. In *Handbook of research on teacher education,* edited by W. R. Houston. Columbus, Ohio: Macmillan.

Bellanca, J. 1995. *Designing professional development for change.* Arlington Heights, Ill.: IRI/SkyLight Training and Publishing.

Ben-Hur, M., ed. 1994. *On Feuerstein's Instrumental Enrichment.* Arlington Heights, Ill.: IRI/SkyLight Training and Publishing.

Berliner, D. C. 1982. Recognizing instructional variables. In *Introduction to education,* edited by D. E. Orlosky. Columbus, Oh.: Merrill.

Berliner, D., and U. Casanova. 1996. *Putting research to work in your school.* Arlington Heights, Ill.: IRI/SkyLight Training and Publishing.

Bernhardt, V. L. 1994. *The school portfolio: A comprehensive framework for school improvement.* Princeton Junction, N.J.: Eye on Education.

Bloom, L., and E. Bacon. 1995. Professional portfolios: An alternative perspective on the preparation of teachers of students with behavioral disorders. *Behavioral Disorders: Journal of the Council for Children with Behavior Disorders* 20 (4): 290-300.

Boileau, D. M. 1993. Scholarship reconsidered: A challenge to use teaching portfolios to document the scholarship of teaching. *JACA* 3 (August–October): 19–24.

Borg, W. R., J. P. Gall, and M. D. Gall. 1993. *Applying educational research: A practical guide.* Third edition. White Plains, N. Y.: Longman.

Bradley, A. 1995a. Overruns spur teacher board to alter plans. *Education Week* 31 May, 1, 12.

———. 1995b. Teacher board providing valuable lessons in using portfolios. *Education Week,* 31 May, 12–13.

———. 1996a. The long haul. *Education Week,* 17 April, 41–48.

———. 1996b. Teaching focus called the key in reform push. *Education Week,* 18 September, 1, 14, 15.

Brandt, R. 1992. On research on teaching: A conversation with Lee Shulman. *Educational Leadership* 49 (7): 14–19.

———. 1996. On a new direction for teacher evaluation: A conversation with Tom McGreal. *Educational Leadership* 53 (6): 30–33.

Brooks, J., and M. Brooks. 1993. *In search of understanding: The case for constructivist classrooms.* Alexandria, Va.: Association for Supervision and Curriculum Development.

Brophy, J. E., and T. L. Good. 1986. Teacher behavior and student achievement. In *Handbook of research on teaching,* edited by M. C. Wittrock. Third edition. New York: Macmillan.

Buday, M. C., and J. A. Kelly. 1996. National board certification and the teaching profession's commitment to quality assurance. *Phi Delta Kappan* 78 (3): 215–19.

Burke, K. 1994. *The mindful school: How to assess authentic learning.* Arlington Heights, Ill.: IRI/SkyLight Training and Publishing.

———, ed. 1996. *Professional portfolios: A collection of articles.* Palatine, Ill.: IRI/SkyLight Training and Publishing.

Burke, K., R. Fogarty, and S. Belgrad. 1994. *The mindful school: The portfolio connection.* Arlington Heights, Ill.: IRI/SkyLight Training and Publishing.

Cameron, D. 1996. The role of teachers in establishing a quality-assurance system. *Phi Delta Kappan* 78 (3): 225–27.

Chapman, C. 1993. *If the shoe fits . . . : How to develop multiple intelligences in the classroom.* Arlington Heights, Ill.: IRI/SkyLight Training and Publishing.

Chance, L., and T. Rakes. 1994. Differentiated evaluation in professional development schools: An alternative paradigm for preservice teacher evaluation. Paper presented at the Create National Evaluation Institute, College of Education, University of Memphis, Gatlinburg, Tennessee. (ERIC Document Reproduction Service No. ED 376 162)

Costa, A. L. 1991. *The school as a home for the mind.* Arlington Heights, Ill.: IRI/SkyLight Training and Publishing.

Costa, A. L., J. Bellanca, and R. Fogarty, eds. 1992. *If minds matter: A foreword to the future.* Vol. 2. Arlington Heights, Ill.: IRI/SkyLight Training and Publishing.

Costa, A. L., and R. J. Garmston. 1994. *Cognitive coaching: A foundation for renaissance schools.* Norwood, Mass.: Christopher-Gordon Publishers.

Csikszentmihalyi, M. 1990. *Flow: The psychology of optimal experience.* New York: Harper Perennial.

Danielson, C. 1996. *Enhancing professional practice: A framework for teaching.* Alexandria, Va.: Association for Supervision and Curriculum Development.

Darling-Hammond, L. 1996. What matters most: A competent teacher for every child. *Phi Delta Kappan* 78 (3): 193–200.

Dietz, M. 1991. *Professional development portfolio: A site-based framework for professional development.* San Ramon, Calif.: Frameworks.

———. 1995. Using portfolios as a framework for professional development. *Journal of Staff Development* 16 (2): 40–43.

Diez, M. 1994. The portfolio: Sonnet, mirror, and map. Keynote presentation at Linking Liberal Arts and Teacher Education: Encouraging Reflection through Portfolios, 6 October. Mission Valley Hilton, San Diego, Calif.

Eisner, E. W. 1985. *The educational imagination: On the design and evaluation of school programs.* Second edition. New York: Macmillan Publishing Co.

———. 1991. *The enlightened eye: Qualitative inquiry and the enhancement of educational practice.* New York: Macmillan Publishing Co.

Ellis, A. K., and J. T. Fouts. 1994. *Research on school restructuring.* Princeton Junction, N.J.: Eye on Education.

Elmore, R. F. 1992. Why restructuring alone won't improve teaching. *Educational Leadership* 49 (7): 44–48.

Elmore, R. F., and Associates. 1990. *Restructuring schools: The next generation of educational reform.* San Francisco: Jossey-Bass, Inc.

Fogarty, R. 1990. *Designs for cooperative interactions.* Arlington Heights, Ill.: IRI/SkyLight Training and Publishing.

———. 1994. *The mindful school: How to teach for metacognitive reflection.* Arlington Heights, Ill.: IRI/SkyLight Training and Publishing.

———. 1995. *Best practices for the learner-centered classroom.* Arlington Heights, Ill.: IRI/SkyLight Training and Publishing.

Fogarty, R., and J. Bellanca. 1993. *Patterns for thinking: Patterns for transfer.* Arlington Heights, Ill.: IRI/SkyLight Training and Publishing.

Fogarty, R., D. Perkins, and J. Barell. 1992. *The mindful school: How to teach for transfer.* Arlington Heights, Ill.: IRI/SkyLight Training and Publishing.

Forte, I., and S. Schurr. 1995. *Making portfolios, products, and performances meaningful and manageable for students and teachers.* Nashville, Tenn.: Incentive Publications, Inc.

Fullan, M. G., with S. Stiegelbauer. 1991. *The new meaning of educational change.* New York: Teachers College Press.

Furtwengler, C. B. 1992. How to observe cooperative learning classrooms. *Educational Leadership* 49 (7): 59–62.

Gellman, E. 1992. The use of portfolios in assessing teacher competence: Measurement issues. *Action in Teacher Education* 14 (4): 39–44.

Glatthorn, A. 1996. *The teacher's portfolio: Fostering and documenting professional development.* Rockport, Mass.: Proactive Publications.

Glickman, C. D. 1991. Pretending not to know what we know. *Educational Leadership* 48 (8): 4–10.

———. 1993. *Renewing America's schools: A guide for school-based action.* San Francisco: Jossey-Bass.

Goodlad, J. I. 1996. Sustaining and extending educational renewal. *Phi Delta Kappan* 78 (3): 228–33.

Hammond, L. 1996. The quiet revolution: Rethinking teacher development. *Educational Leadership* 53 (6): 4–10.

Harp, B. ed. 1994. *Assessment and evaluation for student centered learning.* Second edition. Norwood, Mass.: Christopher-Gordon Publishers.

Hartzell, G. 1995. Helping administrators learn to avoid seven common employee performance appraisal errors. *Journal of Staff Development* 16 (2): 32–35.

Herman, J., P. Aschbacher, and L. Winters. 1992. *A practical guide to alternative assessment.* Alexandria, Va.: Association for Supervision and Curriculum Development.

Hill, B. C., and C. Ruptic. 1994. *Practical aspects of authentic assessment: Putting the pieces together.* Norwood, Mass.: Christopher-Gordon.

Hoerr, T. 1996. Collegiality: A new way to define instructional leadership. *Phi Delta Kappan* 77 (5): 380–81.

Holcomb, E. L. 1996. *Asking the right questions: Tools and techniques for teamwork.* Thousand Oaks, Calif.: Corwin Press—Sage Publications.

Hult, C. Using portfolios to evaluate teachers: Learning from ourselves. *Journal of Teaching Writing* 12 (1): 57–66.

International Reading Association and National Council of Teachers of English. 1996. Standards for the English language, for the profession, by the profession: A guide for discussion. Newark, Del.: IRA—Urbana, Ill.: NCTE.

Jenlink, P., ed. 1995. *Systemic change: Touchstones for the future school.* Arlington Heights, Ill.: IRI/SkyLight Training and Publishing.

Joyce, B., and B. Showers. 1988. *Student achievement through staff development.* New York: Longman.

———. 1996. Staff development as a comprehensive service organization. *Journal of Staff Development* 17 (1): 2–6.

Kimeldorf, M. 1994. *Creating portfolios for success in school, work, and life.* Minneapolis, Minn.: Free Spirit Publishing, Inc.

———. 1996. *A teacher's guide to creating portfolios for success in school, work, and life.* Minneapolis, Minn.: Free Spirit Publishing.

Lieberman, A., ed. 1988. *Building a professional culture in schools.* New York: Teachers College Press.

Lyons, N. 1996. A grassroots experiment in performance assessment. *Educational Leadership* 53 (6): 64–67.

McDonald, J. P., S. Smith, D. Turner, M. Finney, and E. Barton. 1993. *Graduation by exhibition: Assessing genuine achievement.* Alexandria, Va.: Association for Supervision and Curriculum Development.

Millman, J., and L. Darling-Hammond, eds. 1990. *The new handbook of teacher evaluation: Assessing elementary and secondary school teachers.* Newbury Park, Calif.: Sage Publications.

National Commission on Teaching and America's Future. 1996. What matters most: Teaching for America's future. New York: Teachers College, Columbia University.

National Staff Development Council in cooperation with National Association of Secondary School Principals. 1995. *Standards for staff development: High school edition.* Oxford, Ohio: NSDC—Reston, Va: NASSP.

Olson, L. 1996. Leadership standards target teaching, learning. *Education Week* 16 (1): 4, 5.

Patterson, L., J. C. Stansell, and S. Lee. 1990. *Teacher research: From promise to power.* Katonah, N. Y.: Richard C. Owen Publishers.

Perkins, P., and J. Gelfer. 1993. Portfolio assessment of teachers. *Clearing House* 66 (4): 235–37.

Regan, H. 1993. Integrated portfolios as tools for differentiated teacher evaluation: A proposal. *Journal of Personnel Evaluation in Education* 7: 275–90.

Rényi, J. 1996. The longest reform. *Education Week* 16(11): 34, 37.

Rooney, J. 1993. Teacher evaluation: No more "super" vision. *Educational Leadership* 51 (2): 43–44.

Scannell, M., and J. Wain. 1996. New models for state licensing of professional educators. *Phi Delta Kappan* 78 (3): 211–14.

Schmoker, M. 1996. *Results: The key to continuous school improvement.* Alexandria, Va.: Association for Supervision and Curriculum Development.

Searfoss, L., and B. Enz. 1996. Can teacher evaluation reflect holistic instruction? *Educational Leadership* 53 (6): 38–41.

Sergiovanni, T. J. 1990. *Value-added leadership: How to get extraordinary performance in schools.* Orlando, Fla.: Harcourt Brace Jovanovich.

Setteducati, D. 1995. Portfolio self-assessment for teachers: A reflection on the Farmingdale. *Journal of Staff Development* 16 (3): 2–5.

Shanker, A. 1996. Quality assurance: What must be done to strengthen the teaching profession. *Phi Delta Kappan* 78 (3): 220–24.

Showers, B., and B. Joyce. The evaluation of peer coaching. *Educational Leadership* 53 (6): 12–16.

Shulman, L. S. 1988. A union of insufficiencies: Strategies for teacher assessment in a period of educational reform. *Educational Leadership* 46 (3): 36–40.

Smith, S. C., and J. J. Scott. 1990. *The collaborative school: A work environment for effective instruction.* Eugene, Ore.: ERIC—University of Oregon and Reston, Va.: NASSP.

Snyder, J., S. Elliott, N. Bhavnagri, and J. Boyer. 1993. Beyond assessment: University/school collaboration in portfolio review and the challenge to program improvement. *Action in Teacher Education* 15 (4): 55–60.

Sykes, G. 1996. Reform *of* and *as* professional development. *Phi Delta Kappan* 77 (7): 465–67.

Turney, B., and G. Robb. 1971. *Research in education: An introduction.* Hinsdale, Ill.: Dryden Press.

Wise, A. E. 1996. Building a system of quality assurance for the teaching profession: Moving into the 21st century. *Phi Delta Kappan* 78 (3): 191–92.

Wise, A. E., and J. Leibbrand. 1996. Profession-based accreditation: A foundation for high-quality teaching. *Phi Delta Kappan* 78 (3): 202–6.

Wolf, K. 1991. The schoolteacher's portfolio: Issues in design, implementation, and evaluation. *Phi Delta Kappan* 73 (2): 129–36.

———. 1996. Developing an effective teaching portfolio. *Educational Leadership* 53 (6): 34–37.

Wheeler, P. 1993. *Using portfolios to assess teacher performance.* Washington, D.C.: Office of Educational Research and Improvement and Liverware, Calif.: EREAPA Associates.

Index

SkyLight
Training and Publishing Inc.

We Prepare Your Teachers Today
for the Classrooms of Tomorrow

Learn from Our Books and from Our Authors!

Ignite Learning in Your School or District.

SkyLight's team of classroom-experienced consultants can help you foster systemic change for increased student achievement.

Professional development is a process, not an event. SkyLight's seasoned practitioners drive the creation of our on-site professional development programs, graduate courses, research-based publications, interactive video courses, teacher-friendly training materials, and online resources—call SkyLight Training and Publishing Inc. today.

SkyLight specializes in three professional development areas.

Specialty #

1 Best Practices

We **model** the best practices that result in improved student performance and guided applications.

Specialty #

2 Making the Innovations Last

We help set up **support** systems that make innovations part of everyday practice in the long-term systemic improvement of your school or district.

Specialty #

3 How to Assess the Results

We prepare your school leaders to encourage and **assess** teacher growth, **measure** student achievement, and **evaluate** program success.

Contact the SkyLight team and begin a process toward long-term results.

2626 S. Clearbrook Dr., Arlington Heights, IL 60005
800-348-4474 • 847-290-6600 • FAX 847-290-6609
http://www.iriskylight.com

There are
one-story intellects,
two-story intellects, and three-story
intellects with skylights. All fact collectors, who
have no aim beyond their facts, are one-story men. Two-story men
compare, reason, generalize, using the labors of the fact collectors as
well as their own. Three-story men idealize, imagine,
predict—their best illumination comes from
above, through the skylight.

—*Oliver Wendell*

Holmes

SkyLight
Training and Publishing Inc.